WINCHMAN

Chris Murray
Q.G.M

Published by Fledgling Press, 2013
Cover Design: Graeme Clarke
graeme@graemeclarke.co.uk
www.fledglingpress.co.uk

Printed and bound by:
Bell & Bain Limited, Glasgow
ISBN: 9781905916658

ACKNOWLEDGEMENTS

Everyone I have named in this book has been part of my story. I would like to thank them for that – even if I never did quite get round to telling them they would be mentioned.

In particular, a big thank you is due to Clare Cain and her team at Fledgling Press for their efforts. Thanks also to Vicki Maciver, who chose the photo for, and helped design, the cover. I'd also better mention her dad, Iain X Maciver for his help while I was writing this book.

CHAPTER 1

You thought you would pick up this book and read the life story of Chris Murray, eh? Well, sorry to disappoint you. That's not my name. No, no. You haven't picked up the wrong book. Let me explain.

My real name, the one I was christened with, is William Iain Murray. Chris was actually my father's name. Confused? You will be. In the Highlands, and I'm sure elsewhere, people refer to their sons as little versions of the father. So, my father was Big Chris and his eldest son, my older brother Donald, was often known as Wee Chris. Everyone then knew who they were talking about. My birth messed up that cosy arrangement. My brother Donald was no longer Wee Chris but Big Chris and I, although I am now nearly 6ft 2in, became Wee Chris. Still, I was the youngest and that's how it works.

Over the years Donald lost his nickname completely but mine stuck. Except, as I kept growing I was obviously no longer Wee Chris, but Big Chris. It's making your head hurt? Just think how I felt. Why couldn't everyone call me by my correct name? William. So you see, Chris was actually a nickname of sorts, but one which was really only used by people outside our family. It wouldn't feel right if anyone who was related to me called me by that name. They would, of course, always call me William, as would most other people who have known me since I was young.

The other nickname I had back then was The Whale, because my Dad had been a whaler. Not surprisingly perhaps, that was one name I really didn't like. And, of course, because I let them know I hated it, the more the other lads would shout, "Thar she blows!" So, although this book is actually about William Iain Murray and not Chris Murray, I hope you are still interested in learning a bit about my life. That's fine; I have a fair few tales to tell if you bear with me.

How did I come to write this book? Over the years quite a few people had suggested it after hearing yarns about my past adventures. It is perfectly possible these tales were told in the pub and then passed on to others. I dismissed all those suggestions although I knew in the back of my mind that there had been some colourful incidents I could tell people about. As the years crept up on me, I began to realise that people like the late Dr John Macleod of Lochmaddy, who I mention later on in this chapter, may have been right and I should commit my memories to paper.

My hope for this book is that it will be read and understood by the general public and not just by people in the worlds of search and rescue and the military. Therefore, I am going to try and avoid jargon and where it is impossible to do that, I shall try and explain what I mean in plain language. It is my intention to make people smile as well as inform them. Yes, there have been heart-stopping moments in my career as a diver, as well as my 20-odd years dangling on the wire. However, there have also been unusual, thought-provoking and hilarious times too.

I almost came a cropper many times. You will hear how I had to be rescued myself, when I was washed off a boat in the Atlantic; how I was caught as helplessly as an insect on a fly swatter when a pipeline I was diving on, in 140 feet of water, suddenly shot up towards the surface, and how I froze when I realised that my young daughter and I could be wiped out as my dog ran up to us with an unexploded grenade in its mouth.

However, I will also tell you how I set my father's much-loved shed on fire when my daft attempt at making gunpowder went drastically wrong, how I was set on fire myself for other people's fun, how I completely failed to recognise one of the most famous footballers on the planet, and all about the time I came to be caught in a deluge of fresh cow manure from the heavens. Remind me also to tell you how I was shot by some mad, jealous Frenchman who left me for dead in the street.

So, who am I? I reckon it's important to explain where I came from. Firstly, a bit about my family history. My grandfather was the Reverend William Murray. Born in the parish of Little Rogart in the county of Sutherland, his parents also came from there. He was married on June 20, 1905, having known my grandmother, Margaret Sutherland (from Hillview at Rearquhar, in the parish of Dornoch) for some years. Soon after, they went off to Africa where they were both missionaries. In those days the wife had to help the husband and they both set to work in the country we now know as Malawi. In those days, it was known as Nyasaland. They were very busy out there – so busy that they managed to have five sons and one daughter. These were James, David, Willie, John and Christopher, my dad, as well as a daughter, my aunt Marion. She went on to be a nurse and matron who was highly decorated for her work in hospitals and hospital ships around the world.

Being a missionary was a tough existence and there was a constant battle with disease. My grandfather picked up many bugs out there and was often unwell. When Dad was 13, they all came back to Dornoch for an extended holiday due to my grandfather's poor health. My grandfather had just bought a house called Reefton in St Gilbert Street. During his break at home, Grandpa began to show signs of blackwater fever – a disease caused by complications arising after bouts of malaria. His condition deteriorated and he died and was buried in Dornoch. Having lost his father while still just 13, my father then became a pupil at Dornoch Academy. After his school years, not a happy time for him, as I shall explain, he went off to London where he worked for many years in the Smiths clock factory. He then joined the Metropolitan Police and served at various London stations. At one stage, my dad was one of the regular police guards for 10 Downing Street.

Towards the end of World War II, he decided to do his bit in another uniform and joined the Royal Navy, serving on HMS Howe from 1944 to 1945. After the war ended he soon wanted to come back to Scotland and took up forestry work around Dornoch for a time. After a few years he got itchy feet again. Jobs were scarce so it was back to sea, and he joined the whaling ships. He spent several seasons in the Antarctic as a whaler. It was a hard, cold job and when the time came to move on he eventually headed north again and managed to land the job as janitor of Dornoch Academy and then with Grants of Dornoch, the food company. He was at Grants until he retired but sadly died soon afterwards, as a result of injuries he suffered in a car accident.

However, it was when he was in London that my father met mum who was housekeeper to the Tate family, of sugar producers Tate and Lyle. She was Angusina Maclennan who hailed from Marvig in the South Lochs area of the Isle of Lewis. They got together, and before long my older brother Donald, and then myself, put in an appearance. Home was No 16 Maresfield Gardens in mega-posh Hampstead, in the north of the city. I was born in St Mary's Hospital there. Hampstead is still one of the areas with the most millionaires' houses anywhere in the country. I am not sure how or why we ended up living in such a posh area. Maybe it was a police house we had; I never asked.

Our near neighbours, I was told later, were a family called Freud. The family included the famed Clement Freud; the writer and broadcaster, always described as lugubrious, grandson of the psychoanalyst Sigmund Freud and brother of the artist, Lucian Freud. First known as a household name for advertising dog food in a deadpan sort of way on television in the 60s and 70s, Clement then became an MP, a deadpan sort of Liberal MP. Later, of course, he was Sir Clement. We moved back to Scotland when I was just three months old and before long, my younger brother Alasdair was born in Raigmore Hospital in Inverness.

Mum and Dad were good-living people. However, I remember my father being more of a friend than a parent. A brilliant man, he just seemed to touch everyone he came across. Everyone liked him. He didn't smoke but he would certainly take a wee dram on the odd occasion – yes, I do take after Dad in some ways. The old man was full of fun, always cracking jokes and he was a fantastic artist, particularly of cartoons. He was a notable sculptor too, and the type of person who could turn his hand to most things.

Dad also wrote poetry. I remember some of his poems on display at the doctor's surgery. After he died, our next-door neighbour, the late Tom Mackay, gave me a cutting from the Northern Times newspaper of a poem my father had written about the street we lived in.

It is simply called *St Gilbert Street*:

Because of Holy Gilbert's fame
A street was honoured by his name.
The chief street of this ancient town
Where Dornoch worthies sauntered down.
Proud of all that they had done
To make this town a modern one
With Gilbert's street their special pride
Admired throughout the countryside.

But now we hasten to survey
This famous little street today
To see what progress there may be
In this progressive century.
But first of all, you must enquire
Where is this street that you desire?
There is no name-plate there to tell
And maybe it is just as well.
For what you see appears most quaint
If tribute to our patron saint.

If Gilbert Murray now could see
This back street to his memory
A cart-track with uneven crust
Of pot-holes, pools and flying dust;
The likes of which you wouldn't see
In jungle-ringed Trincomalee.
Then would he understand the worry
And chagrin of another Murray.

Life had its challenges, though, for Dad from an early age. He had problems at school in Dornoch which were down to one particular teacher with a drink problem. Some mathematics exam papers he had completed were torn up and thrown in the bin by that teacher so he failed the exam for having 'lost' them.

Yet he was determined that setbacks like that wouldn't hold him back in his life. He did not complain about how he was disadvantaged although he did eventually explain to me why things had not gone so well for him at school.

Of my parents, Dad was the one who was the regular churchgoer. He was also very fond of nature and wildlife and, as any parent would, he also took a great interest in my life and everything I was doing. Yeah, I have very happy memories of my dad. Mum was, well, Mum. She was certainly far stricter than Dad. A smoker all her life, she would never smoke in front of her mother back home in Marvig. It was pretty much taboo back then for island women to puff. She was quite strict towards my older brother although I seem to remember she wouldn't go to church herself as often as my father.

It's true that she wasn't as outgoing as other mums in Dornoch at that time and she kept herself very much to herself. Her great obsession was spending all holidays back in her former home village of Marvig. That was her place, the place of her birth, and her love for it never changed.

I was still in school when I decided I wanted to be either a carpenter or a joiner. When I was 15 I began to wonder whether I should leave school and then I learned of a vacancy at the county council. They were looking for an apprentice joiner.

A job with the council? That's a job for life, everyone said. Well, I applied, got the job and started soon after at the yard in Dornoch. It felt a bit strange going there in my overalls with my piece box but actually knowing very little about joinery. I did have some tools because I had managed to get a grant. The tools cost the princely sum of £15 for the lot, and you know what? I still have them all to this day. After the leisurely atmosphere of the woodwork class in school, where I was really quite good at making small things with wood, going into that workshop with those huge, noisy power tools was very different.

Thankfully, my journeyman, James Matheson, was a fantastic guy who taught me everything he could about the trade. As well as joinery, I was tiling, painting and doing plumbing work as well. I used to make doors, windows and gates from scratch. Apprentices, however, had no electrical tools available to them so I had to do this all by hand. That was an experience. I sure learned the work the hard way. Of course, I made mistakes along the way but that's how you learn properly.

The work largely involved running repairs of all kinds to the various council properties all over the county of Sutherland. If somebody's roof blew off in a gale, we'd go and replace the slates. If pipes had frozen or a boiler had burst, we would be sent. In the morning we could be fitting draught excluders and in the afternoon doing roof repairs. There was no trade union then to say who would do what. You were expected to do everything. Of course, when we did get power tools, things became a lot easier.

As part of my apprenticeship, I had to attend day release, and sometimes block release too, at the Sutherland Technical College in Golspie. It was a fantastic place and even had its own outdoor swimming pool. My brother Donald had gone there before me and told me all about it beforehand. The courses were fairly hard, I suppose. I seem to remember finding them tough going. Some of the teachers could be hard on the students too, but most were far from that. There were some you could even ask for a cigarette and who did treat us very much like adults, although we were still quite young. We were never into any serious drugs – unless you count sex, alcohol, nicotine and rock and roll. They were quite addictive.

The college itself was on the edge of a forest and during the lunch break you could get away from it all by heading into the woodland. I suppose that was when I met and got to know some of the local ladies for the first time. Some even became girlfriends of mine for a time. Ah yes, I remember those lunchtimes very well.

My friends and I lived for the weekend. Every Friday we headed off to a dance somewhere. It wasn't that we had to go far. There was usually a dance in Golspie or sometimes in the Burghfield Hotel in Dornoch. Now and again, we might even go further afield and head for the bright lights of Helmsdale. Or Tain, when there was a free bus. Occasionally, we might even go to the Strathpeffer Pavilion. There was usually a show on most weekends.

If the Maurice Lynch Showband, an Irish band which seemed to be constantly touring in Scotland, was appearing in Wick or Thurso, we might even take the bus up there. Those four or five years of my apprenticeship were a very enjoyable time for me and I learned a lot. I even managed to learn a bit about being a joiner too.

I had a friend, Graham Grant, known as Goondy, who was a slaughterman in Dornoch. His father, Angus, was the head gamekeeper on the Torrish Estate, out near Helmsdale. We would go over there some weekends, often with Jimmy Bain, the under-keeper, when there were big shoots for grouse or woodcock, or even to do some salmon fishing on the river. We would be supplied with guns and would go out on the estate with Angus and Jimmy. Although I didn't mind shooting birds, I didn't really take to killing four-legged beasts. Most of the estate people were really very good to us and we would often be given some of the day's kill to take home. A rare treat. After the shoot, of course, we would all pile back to the gamekeeper's house and, in accordance with Highland tradition, the alcohol would flow. Those parties would go on to the wee small hours and some of them were really quite wild. It was quite an eye-opener, living it up with some very well-off people and, even now, it would not really be appropriate to go into too much detail about what actually happened at some of those estate dos. The guests would come from all around Europe and were paying a lot of money for their week's shooting and fishing. When I did manage to get an invitation to their late-night parties which often went on to 6am, I rarely said no. Funny that.

Home in Dornoch was, of course, Reefton in Saint Gilbert Street, then just a cobblestone and dust path. The house was named after some place in South Africa, or maybe New Zealand, where my grandfather had been. One of my earliest memories is of the time I went missing when I was little more than a toddler. Snow was falling heavily and search parties looked for me for two hours without success. Eventually I made my own way back to the house where I was quizzed about where I had been. All I remembered was the snow swishing around me and falling into a snowdrift at one point. It was all just good fun to me.

Dad decided that it was better dealing with me one-to-one. He took me upstairs, away from everyone else, and asked where the heck I had been. I looked at him earnestly and then I made up the most fantastic tale about a big wind which had come down and swept me up, up and away. There was nothing I could do about it, I told him. Poor Dad, that wasn't quite the explanation he had been looking for. I was only three or four years old and many a time since then he reminded me of the tale I came up with which I thought would keep me out of trouble.

Growing up in Dornoch was a happy time for me. I got up to all sorts of mischief although I can't say I actually enjoyed school that much. I didn't really knuckle down to it and I suppose I was a bit of a big softie. I was bullied a bit but I do think I brought much of it on myself by talking back to people. School was Dornoch Primary and then Dornoch Academy. A lot of my friends at that time came down from the west coast of Sutherland and stayed during the week in the hostel in Dornoch. I was not what you would call academic. In fact, I ended up in a 'P' class – I think that stood for Practical. It meant we were offered a lot of practical classes instead of academic and I really took to metalwork and woodwork. That's where I was happiest.

Quite a few of my friends also ended up in the 'P' class. For some of them that proved no hindrance at all and they went on to have academic careers. I am still in touch with some of my former classmates and there is even a professor or two among them. My memories of my teachers are all really very positive. I can't think of any I had problems with. They pretty much all went out of their way to help me. I was the problem. At that stage, I just didn't want to learn anything other than practical subjects. I just couldn't see the value of academic subjects although, of course, my opinion has changed a lot over the years and now I often wish I had applied myself more.

When I was 13, I joined the Army Cadets. That was something different which I found exciting. There was a uniform to wear and exciting activities too, like rifle shooting. We did a lot of that at Fort George and I did well in competitions with the .303 rifle – quite a number of times Cadet Murray came home with medals for shooting, destined for the sideboard. While I was still in school I went with the cadets to Nijmegen, Holland, to do a four-day, 100-mile march – another new experience: meeting people from other nations and seeing how they lived. We all finished the march and received a medal to confirm it. I'm not quite sure where that gong is now but I do have many happy memories of going Dutch.

*

For some time my dad worked on the Royal Dornoch Golf Course as a greenkeeper. During the summer he was usually up about 4am or 5am to make sure that the greens were fit and ready for those who were paying a lot of money to play on the course. The bunkers had to be raked and there was always mowing to be done; always lots to do. When I was in school and Dad was working there, I used to get up early too, to go round the golf course with him.

It was a beautiful spot, just beside the Dornoch beach and I used to envy my dad – although it wasn't always lovely weather – we had some horrible rainy days too, but the work had to be done just the same. Dad was always jovial, whistling or singing a song to himself, and round he would go. He would tell me all kinds of stories about people he met on the golf course. He was told one particular day before he went to work that someone had lost a highly expensive watch. When I say highly expensive, it was worth thousands of pounds and that's going back a good number of years. Dad being Dad, said he would look for it. He went right to the end of the 18-hole course towards Embo and on the way back had to answer a call of nature. He went into a secluded bunker to have a wee Jimmy Riddle. Now my dad would never tell tales or anything like that. He was very straight in the way he recounted events. As he was piddling away, the stream uncovered a watch in the bunker. He couldn't believe his eyes. He cleaned it off and took it back to the clubhouse. It was indeed the watch which this person had lost – there was a chance in a million something like that could have happened. He also came across a gent's gold wedding ring once, as he was raking a bunker.

A particular TV and film celebrity often seen around the Dornoch area when we were young was the actor James Robertson Justice; best known for films like *Doctor In the House*, where he was Sir Lancelot Spratt, and *Chitty Chitty Bang Bang*. James lived in the area known as Spinningdale, where there are maybe twenty houses beside the ruined and dilapidated mill buildings, down by the shore. A regular visitor to Dornoch and the surrounding villages, James was a real sportsman in his own right.

He used to frequent the grouse moors outside the Dornoch area with his falcons. How he loved showing them off to anyone who had the time to listen to him When I was in Dornoch Primary, I think I must have been seven or eight years old, I remember walking back from school with friends when we met up with James Robertson Justice outside the Eagle Hotel: a big hotel covered in ivy, and this meeting still sticks in my mind.

We were merely little fellows and at that time he was the biggest man on the whole planet – as far as we were concerned anyway. Along with his beard and his immense personality, he also had this incredible booming voice which seemed to resound right through the town of Dornoch. Despite that, he was a fantastic, friendly and interesting guy to us youngsters. We knew he was famous at the time because we were told so by the grown-ups. That made it all the more exciting. Everybody talked about him – and he chose to live in our town. It was great to meet him with his big leather gloves and straps which were attached to the falcon as it perched on his arm, usually with a hood over its head.

We would be allowed to pet the falcon while he regaled us with his colourful tales. These were always stories about his prowess at hunting, how the falcons would bring down the grouse and how he would go about retrieving them afterwards. One story he told us was that some lord or laird was out on the hill shooting for grouse and one of his servants got excited when a grouse took off in the long heather. The problem was that he had a stammer. He began shouting, "A grace, your grouse," getting himself so worked up that the words came out all wrong.

We were in stitches listening to stories like that. And I believe it was a true story although I am not sure who the lord or laird was – probably the Duke of Sutherland, so that would be going back a bit.

A biography by James Hogg, called *James Robertson Justice: What's The Bleeding Time?* came out in 2008 and I learned that James was actually a bit of a rogue. The glamorous lady we always saw with him was not, in fact, his wife at all. He was living in Spinningdale with a mistress, an actress called Irina von Meyendorff. There are a few mysteries about him still. Why did he pretend to be Scottish? He told everyone, even on TV shows, that he was born in a distillery on the Isle of Skye. That was all nonsense – he was actually a Londoner.

However, he did speak many languages fluently, including Gaelic. His real wife eventually sued him for much of his money and Mr Hogg's book says Spinningdale had to be sold on the orders of the bankruptcy court. In all, James appeared in 87 films and in some his name appears as Seamus Mòr na Feusag, which is Gaelic for Big James with the Beard. Maybe he learned it when he was filming *Whisky Galore* on Barra? The sad endnote is that Mr Hogg says James died penniless in 1975, just days after finally marrying Ms von Meyendorff. Broke perhaps, but he was also said to have been happy at the end. Well, he was nice to us and made us happy too. Aye, I raise my glass to James Robertson Justice.

There were amazing parallels between James Robertson and another man I met in Uist. The late Dr John Macleod, of Lochmaddy, was the first person to tell me I should write this book. John too, had been a diver, when he did his national service in Malta between 1957 and 1959. I hope Lorna and the family will forgive me for suggesting that Dr John looked a bit like James Robertson Justice. The likeness was such that people in Uist would often say that the part of the rural doctor that James, as Dr Maclaren, played so splendidly in the film *Whisky Galore,* was a bit like Dr John with his own country practice in North Uist.

As I got older, my main interest became fishing. Any chance I had I would be away on one of the local lochs with my friends. I recall a day I was on my own on Loch Beannach, outside Lairg in the county of Sutherland, when I remembered seeing the remains of old boatsheds there when I was younger. I thought the bottom of the loch would be a good place to find some old-fashioned bottles. I got my wetsuit on and instead of carrying weights with me, I used a big boulder to weigh myself down. The clarity of the water was good and after being down for a short while, I heard the noise of an outboard in the loch. I hadn't realised there was anybody around but they sounded like they were round the headland from where I was. I was a bit concerned as on this particular loch guests paid quite a lot of money to go fishing for the large trout. If I upset these people then it wasn't going to look very good for me, and I am afraid that's precisely what happened. The outboard engine stopped but I couldn't actually see a boat although the water was clear – just not clear enough to see to the surface.

The toffs had come round to their favourite fishing spot, shut down the engine and were using the oars to fly-fish. I waited until I thought they had gone. I couldn't hold my breath any longer and headed to the surface. Had I known there was anybody in the loch, I would have kept well away from that area. I broke the surface amid a lot of boiling bubbles and emerged right beside their boat. My sudden appearance gave the genteel fishermen a terrible fright. By the look of them, they nearly suffered heart attacks. They thought it was some monster from the deep – a huge, black-headed creature with a slithery black tongue snaking out of its mouth up to the top of its head. Yeeeaggghhh! That was just my snorkel, of course.

The women were absolutely petrified and were screaming their heads off. I thought, 'What's the point trying to explain, I'm off.' As I swam for the shore, I could hear their shrieks and the ghillie on the boat cursing after me. On the bank, I got my mask off and called over to apologise profusely and explain that I hadn't realised they were there. The ghillie was furious, even when I explained I wouldn't have been there had I known. I had ruined the fishing for everybody for the day in this part of the loch, he said. All I could do was say sorry but he told me not to use that bloody loch again. "Now clear off!" he yelled. I did scarper but I did go back to that loch on other occasions – although I always made doubly sure there were no stroppy ghillies around first.

Sometimes I fell foul of the law over poaching, or should I say, alleged poaching? Ach, there was nothing alleged about it. I was quite partial to a bit of fresh salmon and fresh pheasant too. Unfortunately, my own finances did not allow me to buy such luxuries from the shops. Happily, it just so happened that the River Evelix ran just outside Dornoch and I would go there with my gaff and fox snare, which is just like a rabbit snare but bigger. I would just swim up behind the salmon and loop it over the tail. It was easier if there was someone with you to haul the fish in but I could manage on my own with a tether which was excellent for catching big fish like that. One or two salmon would be taken – but only for the pot, you understand.

One day I somehow caught more of the king of fish than I had expected to. No bag big enough could be found so I put them into my camouflage jacket and carried them in that. It was pretty heavy and normally, with salmon secreted about my person, I would have skirted round the edge of town so that I was less likely to bump into anyone, but the weight of this haul was so tiring that I just walked the last mile on the main road.

Before I had gone very far, a Land Rover pulled up and in it was the local bobby, John Cameron. Oh no! Of all people to offer me a lift. I obviously looked knackered and he insisted I get in. I didn't want to but I also didn't want to draw attention to myself by refusing. That was awkward, me sitting there beside the constable as I tried to hide the scales on my jacket and trousers.

He soon asked what I had in the jacket. I said it was 'bioraichean', the Gaelic for dogfish, as well as some turnips I was taking to a friend. I could see the suspicion etched into his face. After all, there must have been something wrong with his nose if he was not catching that distinctive salmon smell. When he dropped me off at the Eagle Hotel, he had a smirk on his face and said I would need a dram after lugging that jacket about. I would indeed, I agreed.

"Well, you enjoy it, and whatever else you have in there," he said with a smile, and an obvious emphasis on the "whatever else".

However, I was caught in possession of salmon once. That was also on the River Evelix but at a different pool. Again, I was using a fox snare to catch salmon by the tail. I would just slip quietly into the river and under the water. When I'd see a salmon tail fluttering I would slowly swim up behind it and hook the snare round its tail before yanking it tight. If I had a friend on the bank, I would hand them the snare and they would pull it in. Being on my own, I had to drag the fish ashore by myself. It was a good day that one and I got five; I was very chuffed with myself.

Just after I had put the fish in the boot of my car, a moped came along. 'Oh no,' I thought. 'That's all I need.' It was a policeman by the name of Angus Mackay. They called him Angus Gashegy, after the place where he stayed.

"What are you up to today, Chris?" he asked.

"Ach, I was just in for a wee swim." I told him I was hoping to find some freshwater mussels and get some pearls. At that time, you were allowed to do that sort of thing.

Angus was immediately suspicious, seeing me there in my black wetsuit − like something out of the SAS. He wanted to see the pearls and the shells of the mussels I had tried.

"No, I didn't find any pearls and I just threw the shells back in," I lied. He wasn't having it. He made me open the boot of the Ford Corsair and there they were. Five beauties. Some negotiation took place, warnings were issued and I gave him one of the salmon for himself. However, he still wanted to know how I had caught them.

I told him about the fox snare and he then wanted to know about the wetsuit and whether I had another one. I said I did, but wasn't sure if it would fit him, what with his beer belly and all that. However, I went home and got it for him anyway. I explained that it was a two-piece and that the jacket part had a jockstrap arrangement that went up and under, if you know what I mean. He said he understood but he had never been in a river after a salmon before so he knew nothing about wetsuits.

I heard later about Angus's first expedition with his newly-acquired swimwear. He caught nothing, apparently, and I would guess that was because he made so much noise getting into the water. That wasn't all, though. When he had got out of the water, Angus had got stuck in the suit. He couldn't undo the studs because, well, he didn't have a clue and he was going about it completely the wrong way. Unfortunately, I wasn't there to help him and before long he needed the toilet. Time was of the essence. He had to cut himself out of the dashed thing. That must have been so funny to watch. I really wish I had been there. The next time I saw Angus, he was not a happy chap. He said he would never be trying that particular method of getting one for the pot. Oh, well, more for the rest of us . . .

On the odd occasion, I was known to acquire some ducks and pheasants − for the pot too, you understand. This day, I was going past the Middle Ferry, outside Embo on the Cambusmore Estate, when someone saw my car and reported that I had been shooting ducks. I had my legal gun in the car but it wasn't me who had been shooting, I swear. Before I knew what was happening, the gamekeeper's 4x4 was up behind me, flashing his lights to try and get me to stop. 'No way,' I thought. 'I've done nothing wrong.'

He continued behind me all the way up to Dornoch and to the police station where my girlfriend Shona worked. In fact, it was her car I was driving that day. The gamey made a right old scene when we got up there. He rushed out of his wagon like something out of an American cop show and was trying to scramble up the grassy bank to get to the car I was in when he fell flat on his face. He looked ridiculous but demanded the inspector come out to search my car for pheasants and ducks. He was convinced there was game in the car. I was saying nothing, of course – I knew I was innocent. I just found it very funny that this guy was making such a plonker of himself.

Shona turned up in uniform and asked what was going on. I told her I was accused of poaching.

"Would I do such a thing, Shona?"

She thought it best not to answer that one. After about 10 minutes, I let them search the car and there wasn't even a feather in it. You should have seen the disappointment on the gamekeeper's face. He was not pleased. After that, he went out of his way to try to catch me but I never let that happen. I suppose I was just a bit smarter than he was. When Shona calmed down, she saw the funny side too. I learned my lesson after that experience, however. Whenever I did go poaching, I was just a little bit more careful.

In my early teens I discovered air rifles and that meant non-stop target practice around the village. As the years rolled on, I will not pretend I got any wiser. Some of us graduated to making our own gunpowder. I would go to the ironmonger and buy weedkiller, and my friend would go to the chemist and buy flowers of sulphur. I would make charcoal, a vital ingredient, in little tins, and perfected the technique of making both fast powder and slow powder. Anything we wanted. It was easy to make.

Then the fun would start. We set up small explosions, just for a laugh, and then moved onto bows and arrows. However, these arrows had explosive heads on them. You might think that was a tad dangerous. And you'd be right. Encouraged by the fact that we seemed to have a knack for it, us lads then moved up to the manufacture of sky rockets, no less. We would put our homemade gunpowder into old grease guns and make fuses. That would send the grease guns hundreds of feet in the air. We knew it was very wrong and that there was a possibility of something very bad happening, but it was also very thrilling. Ach, we had a lot of fun – until the day it all went wrong.

The manufacturing process, such as it was, was carried out in the shed at the back of Reefton. This particular day I was testing how long one of the fuses took to burn. Suddenly, it spat sparks into an open jar of gunpowder. The gunpowder didn't actually explode because it wasn't compressed but it caught fire and burned fiercely, shattering the jar and sending fiery debris everywhere. This quickly set light to the floor and the walls. In minutes, the entire shed was ablaze with all my dad's precious equipment and tools in it. There was nothing I could safely do. I really didn't know which was going to be most dangerous – fighting the fire or facing the wrath of my father. I managed to douse some of the flames but, oh heck, there was an awful lot of damage. There was no way to hide it either. I'd burnt my fingers trying to get to get the fizzing gunpowder out of the shed and, in any case, the pall of smoke could be seen for miles away. People from around Dornoch started rushing over to see what had happened. What could I do? I lied through my teeth, of course. I was just burning rubbish. All under control, I said. Nothing to worry about. However, when my parents got home they weren't so easily fooled and they soon realised what I had been up to. There was an almighty row.

So, having been banned from bomb-making and explosives-handling of all kinds, my friends and I sought other pursuits. That, I'm sure, is when my interest in off-road motorcycles began. There were still a lot of old Norton, BSA and Matchless wartime motorbikes that crofters often had lying in their barns. We would relieve them of these machines, sometimes for just a fiver, and do them up for us to go scrambling on the moors, hills and beaches. Learning how to strip them down was fun. That initial engineering experience helped me many times in later life. If we couldn't get the bike to work, we just took it apart and started all over again. Most of the bikes we just trashed to destruction and they often ended up in the dump at the back of a local farmyard. And then someone had the fantastic idea of trying to blow up of one of these bike engines. After destroying my old man's shed, I wasn't very keen but I thought, 'Hey, this could be fun.' So I said OK, one more time. We got an engine – from a single-cylinder 500cc Norton, I think it was. Having got the cylinder to bottom dead centre and filled half the chamber with gunpowder, we bored a spark plug with wires through it and screwed it up tight.

Up the hill we called Leathad na Searmag, we dug a big hole in the ground, about 100 yards from a derelict building. We got a six-volt battery which had a switch on it, and attached the wires from that onto the engine. Then a fishing line about 100 yards long was attached to the switch and fed back into the building. Tossing a coin to see who was going to pull the switch, it fell to me. There was not so much a bang but a low, muffled 'boomph'. The shock wave, however, was tremendous. All I can remember is running for our lives as earth and stones flew all around us. When the dust settled, we crept out and found a crater that was six feet deep and probably eight feet across. The only piece we ever found of that engine was one valve. The rest had been incinerated and catapulted to all the four corners. That was it. We learned our lesson after that fright. No more explosives for us. We just stuck with motorbikes till we were old enough to have cars. Thankfully, we were unhurt but it was one heck of a lesson about how careful you have to be with explosives. Yet another lesson that was to be very useful later in my life . . .

My job with the county was mainly working on council houses. We would be erecting fences, doing drainage work, roofing, tiling and repairing storm damage. It wasn't just joinery work we were expected to do either. Jacks of all trades is what we were and we'd work all around the county of Sutherland. There was a lot of hard graft involved. However, I still had to be trained properly in carpentry and joinery at the technical college in Golspie and I did manage to pass my City and Guilds.

I remember, one day in the workshop, I was cutting up a 6 x 2 plank and the aluminium guard on top of the circular saw wasn't as tight as it should have been. Yes, I should have checked that before I started on the work. Halfway through, I noticed the guard falling and there was nothing I could do apart from drop everything and duck. On the way down I hit the red stop button at the side of the saw. I did that just as the guard dropped, there was a hell of a bang and everything came to a stop.

I looked at the blade and the guard. The guard was peppered with holes, the teeth from the saw had come right through the guard and the door behind me was peppered with shards of metal. Some of them had penetrated right through the door. If I had been standing there at that time I would certainly have been maimed or even killed. A sharp lesson for me, to always make sure that safety comes first in any sort of job like that. When the guard on that saw was replaced, it was a spring-loaded one so that the same sort of incident couldn't happen again.

There have been one or two other close shaves in my life. I had a severe medical emergency, a near thing or two as I was diving and I was thrown into the Atlantic from a ship, in a violent storm. Oh, yes, and someone shot me at close range in a street in France. More on these incidents later, but you know something? I still shiver when I think of what could have happened with that circular saw.

My apprenticeship lasted four years and I then became a full tradesman joiner. During the time I was serving my apprenticeship my brother Donald was sending me postcards and letters from all around the world. He had joined the Royal Navy when he was 15 years old and started off in HMS Ganges, a shore base in Ipswich where he did his initial training, moving from there to aircraft carriers to continue his engineering training. At that time he was on HMS Victorious. The more of these postcards I got, the more I wanted to leave Dornoch and join the Royal Navy myself, to see a bit of the world and get a bit of excitement. Enjoyable though my work as a joiner was, I just had the wanderlust, so I decided once I had finished my joinery stint that was what I wanted to do. I didn't waste any time and applied to join up to serve my Queen and country at the careers office in Bridge Street, Inverness. I was accepted and in December of 1971 I signed on the dotted line. Straight away, I was sent to HMS Raleigh down in Cornwall for basic training and the start of a new and different life.

CHAPTER 2

My first few weeks in the navy in 1971 were really what I'd been led to expect – lots of square-bashing. You were told how to iron your uniform – some of us had never seen an iron in our lives before and some couldn't even wash a hanky. It was no big deal to me, I could cope with that alright, but for some of the lads it was hell on earth. All about hygiene, cleanliness and our own appearance, as well as our ability to obey all orders to the letter. If you couldn't follow those simple rules, you were going to have difficulties throughout your service in the Royal Navy. It was obvious a lot of the guys weren't going to make it anyway because they had no discipline and they weren't going to listen to orders from any senior instructors or officers.

At the same time we were also out orienteering and on marches, runs, and shooting training. It was also at Raleigh that I got my first introduction to diving. You know what? I liked it. After basic training I was asked what I would like to do in the Royal Navy. We were given a choice of trades involving anti-submarine warfare, gunnery, engineering, as well as electrical trades etc. And there was diving. That was my number one choice.

As I have said, my introduction to diving was actually at HMS Raleigh itself. The first thing I had to do was an aptitude test in the swimming pool and this was just swimming. No actual diving was involved but I had to get through what was a pretty stringent swimming test. I was by no means a brilliant swimmer and I am still not a brilliant swimmer compared to some guys on the course who could do double flips on the high board. I struggled with a lot of the tests but managed most of them. Once, I had to tread water with a weight belt round my waist. I was having difficulty keeping afloat and, in fact, I was starting to sink; I was sinking to the bottom, pushing myself to the surface, getting a few gulps of air, back down to the bottom, and every time I came up the surface I could see all these young guys laughing, tears running down their faces. They thought it was so funny while I was having a hell of a hard time.

Eventually, I had to be taken up and I was sick on the side of the swimming pool. Once I got over that I asked the instructor if I could go back in again. He said, "Yes, carry on. I want you to do two runs of the pool, backstroke, with the weight belt on." I think I managed around one and a half runs when he asked me to tread water again. I began treading water and the same thing happened again; down I went, up again and I was sick on the side of the pool. I was a sorry heap in the corner and I felt really miserable. The Chief Diver who was taking the aptitude test said, "Come and see me up in my office when the swimming bit is finished." The boys were saying, "Sorry Chris, looks like you've messed this one up." They were wishing me all the best with my career in whatever I wanted to do.

Into the Chief Diver's office I went and he asked me what I thought I was doing in the pool. I replied that as far as I was concerned, I was doing my best to get through an aptitude test for diving. He then said I was pretty good under the water and that I had spent far more time under the water than I had on the surface. 'True,' I thought.

He said, "Let me tell you something. See those guys who were out there laughing at you when you were doing the test, they will be lucky if two or three of them, at the most, get through the course." He explained they were looking for triers and not fantastic swimmers.

"All these fellows are fantastic swimmers but that doesn't mean they are going to get through this course. Between you and me," he said, "I am actually putting you through for the diving course." Wow.

I understood what he was saying. I didn't say anything to the rest of the guys but they were very surprised I was still on the course. Some of them didn't get through the course because they thought they were God's gift and and mouthed off all the time but, don't get me wrong, I was no angel myself. I just knew when to belt up.

At HMS Raleigh my instruction continued, learning about all aspects of diving and diving equipment. We were sent to the static ponds: just watering holes for the fire service, which were about 15 feet deep and black as night. There was a lot of muck in them and we were sent down into these holes with a hammer and chisel and a few links of chain which we had to cut – after finding something to cut the links with. We also had to assemble some valves, all more or less done by touch because of the visibility – or lack of it.

After two or three hours, we would be really cold with aching arms but we continued until told to come out of the water. If someone came out before then, because he decided he didn't like it or whatever, he was off the course. It was pretty mucky and horrible down there but I got through it. Some did not. From there we went into open water and I did my first dive at a place called Jupiter Point. Soon, it became second nature for me to get into the water. It was all part of the aptitude course, from the basic swimming part to learning how to dive in open water. Before the course even started, a few of the guys failed to make the grade and they had to go on to other trades.

We were then sent to Portsmouth, to a place called Horsea Island. There was a man-made lake and that's where we spent the rest of the time on the course. We were billeted in HMS Vernon which no longer exists. It's a shopping centre now, I believe. Each day we attended that very strange and difficult clearance diving course. The instructors all seemed sadistic to me and I am sure they had to be pretty tough to get guys like us through it. We were introduced to CDBA (Clearance Divers Breathing Apparatus), and SDDE (Surface Demand Diving Equipment). We also used attack sets: breathing sets using pure oxygen. These are the type which do not produce bubbles when used.

Using underwater compasses, rendezvous points were set up and we had to navigate under the water at any time, day or night, until it became second nature to us. Those instructors were never bloody happy. Even when we were in bed thunderflashes would sometimes be thrown through the windows and an instructor would shout "Awkward!" I don't know why that word was used but it became second nature to get up, or stop whatever we were doing, and get into a suit immediately. We had to get our skates on and be ready in two minutes, with all our diving gear and into the water. That could happen at any time – day or night. We had small booster pumps and gas transfer was done by hand, from one main bottle to the smaller diving bottles. Very hard work it was, too. We might be halfway through that and get another instruction to strip off and jump off the board which was about 40 feet high, and into the water, swim round the lake starkers and then complete a gruelling run with perhaps a telegraph pole carried between us.

That could last for an hour until we were absolutely knackered – and then they would shout "Awkward!" and it would be back into our suits and into the water again. This could go on for hours and hours until we were completely exhausted. Awkward? I'll say it was bloody awkward. When we were diving during the day, we were only allowed soup and bread. We couldn't have anything more than that in case we had cramps or got sick, but we'd have a proper meal at night.

'Live-in Week' at Horsea Island was the final seven days of the course. During that week we had to endure something which a lot of people may not entirely understand – 'mud runs'. That was when we went into a creek, as we called it. We would be up to our waists in gunge; crawling through slime for perhaps up to two hours, to get from one point to another, with thunderflashes (small explosive charges, thrown at us in mock combat) raining down on us. Those that didn't make it through were told to stay there until such time as they did. It was really difficult, very hard going and some of the places we were sent to, like the mudflats in the tidal estuaries, were full of rats and glass so we had to wrap lots and lots of clothing round our boots and hands. Whoever came last in the mud run would have to be helped by the guy at the front. He had to go back and they'd be tied together until such time as they reached the finishing line, regardless of how long it took. Everyone had to do it and if one guy didn't complete it, the rest would have to do it again. The system was sadistic, I thought.

During these runs we would be wearing drysuits. That was why the runs were known as 'boil-in-the-bag'. It was unbelievably hot. When we eventually did complete the run, we were sent to the lake to wash the mud off and cool down. This went on day and night during live-in week. It was a form of torture, really, but I was never so fit in my whole life. A few of the boys cracked up during that period and it was becoming apparent who were more likely to get through.

There was also a lot of theory work in the classroom after the practical diving was done. It was happy days when I passed that course. I think sixteen of us passed out of around thirty that began. It was a very proud moment for me when I was issued with my diver's badge after finishing course ECD9A and qualifying as a basic clearance diver.

During the 'live-in week' we also had to go down to a place called Fareham Creek where HMS Eagle, an old aircraft carrier, was mothballed. We were taken alongside and had to jump off the flight deck into the water – a long, long way down. Just looking down gave us butterflies in our stomachs but we had to jump. We used to shout "Geronimo!" as we leapt off and hit the water like a bullet, climb up the anchor chain and repeat the process all over again. Having done that twice, we then had to swim to the mud on Fareham Creek and carry out mud runs for about an hour before getting back into the water and back to the aircraft carrier. After all that, it was very difficult to climb up the anchor chain because we were muddy, slimy, sweaty and knackered. It wasn't easy.

All this was our daytime exercise. At night, on HMS Eagle and some of the other ships based there, we used to have to perform a 'bracelet', as it was called. This involved a bottom search of one of the ships which were so vast we could get lost underneath. There could be a foot to sixteen inches of weed growing underneath them and somebody would have planted a limpet mine somewhere among the acres of steel which we were supposed to find. We were all joined together by little arm-bands with Inglefield clips on them. We formed this bracelet from stem to stern and we had to somehow find the little limpet mine. It was all done on air, and also mixed gas diving. Being clearance divers, we had to learn about explosives, detonators, fuses and Cordtex as well as how to use them in a manner that was safe to ourselves and others. The main bomb and mine disposal courses came later.

The gases we used were nitrogen and oxygen. We used different mixes; for example 60/40 was 60 per cent oxygen and 40 per cent nitrogen. You could dive to max 82 feet on that. On 40/60 you could dive 140 feet and with 32.5/67.5 you could dive to 180 feet. Also, there was pure oxygen, known as O2, as you may remember if you did chemistry in school, but we couldn't dive to more than 33 feet on this because we were likely to get oxygen poisoning. We did a lot of training on pure O2 for attack swimming and placing limpet mines on the hulls of a ships. The strange thing is, that although most people can take pure O2 to a max depth of 33ft, there are some who cannot.

I remember one of the team was using his attack set on a guide-line at around 20 feet deep. He was ahead of me and, after a few minutes, I suddenly realised he was on the bottom. I thought he was mucking around. He seemed to be dancing all over the place on the seabed. Shall we have a wee boogie down here? I didn't register for a few seconds that he was actually convulsing. I managed to get him to the surface and have him taken ashore. He was okay afterwards but the reason for the fit was his low O2 tolerance. He was just one of the few people who couldn't take O2 under pressure – so he was another guy off the course. There was no way he could continue.

I mentioned Cordtex a while back. This is an explosive in the form of a rope like a washing line. It comes in spools of hundreds of feet. There are many different uses for Cordtex, for example, if we wanted to take the propeller off a submarine. If there were no carbon seals on the propellor then we could use a few turns of Cordtex on the propeller shaft and just blow it. It was not going to cause any damage but would loosen the prop so we could get it off. The normal burn rate for Cordtex is about 21,000 feet a second. That's right – four miles a second. It can be used in lots of different ways. It's an explosive in itself but was often used to detonate another substance like, for example, a plastic explosive. Plastic explosive can be moulded like plasticine to make shaped charges. Plastic, or PE as we called it, was very handy stuff to work with but if you were moulding it, it was best to keep your hands away from your face as it could give you a tremendous headache because of the chemicals it contained. I am not sure if they still use this in the Royal Navy nowadays, or something more potent.

Many people may think you have to go into the guts of mines and bombs to get the fuses out and that might be true in some cases. However, under normal circumstances in the trade that I was in, if we came across a Mark 17 floating mine for instance, around the Western

Isles, which happened many times, we would fit a 5lb plastic explosive pack onto the side of the mine, set a timer and blow it. Some of these mines were rusted so badly you couldn't tell if they were dummy mines or if they were live, but we would blow them up anyway.

One of the benefits of being in the navy was several weeks of leave each year. Because Mum was from Marvig on Lewis, that wee village in South Lochs was a special place for our family. A very good friend of mine there was Hector Macdonald, known as Hector Fido. Hector was a well-known songwriter and also one of the few survivors of the armed merchant ship Rawalpindi when she was blown to bits by the battleships Scharnhorst and Gneisenau, north of the Faeroes in 1939. He had a weaving shed and was always on the loom or fish farming. He liked a wee dram, did Hector. On leave once, I went to see him and found him in the shed. This one time I had brought a couple of bottles of Glenfiddich. He said thanks, and without another word unscrewed the lids of both and poured them into the tank of a Seagull outboard engine hanging on the wall.

"What on earth are you doing?" I asked.

"You'll see in a minute, Willie," he said. I watched as he undid the tube coming from the fuel tank, opened the valve and filled his nip glass and mine from the tube. With a wink, he said, "No one is going to think of looking in here." He then patted the engine whilst peeking to see that no one was around. I couldn't believe it. Hector had flushed out and cleaned the fuel tank and tubes of the outboard engine so he could store his secret stash of whisky in it. He was right. No one ever thought of checking the outboard. No one ever found out where it was except the two of us. I must admit I looked forward to my visits to see Hector in Marvig.

I joined my first ship, HMS Kedleston − a wooden minehunter, at Newcastle. We were on board for a year, to learn about clearance diving and how to deal with bombs and mines. One of our main jobs was searching for mines, but we also learned about fishery protection. We had sonar on board which could detect mines and, once a mine was detected, a rubber dinghy would be launched. Slung under this was an explosive device, an actual bomb connected to cables and timers.

My grandparents, William and Margaret Murray

Aunt Marion in her uniform

My parents, Chris and Agnes Murray

Chris Murray at Faslane, 1973 Diving team

Chris throwing the hammer, Invercarron Highland Gathering, 1980

Diver Chris Murray getting rather hot at Crinnan, 1973

Just a young sailor boy!

Lawry Lawrence doing what a diver does best, 1974

RN Diver Chris Murray overheating at Scrabster

Under the direction of the skipper on the bridge, we would be sent in the direction of the suspected mine. The skipper would tell us by radio when to drop the explosive device and, as long as it was released within a few feet of the ground mine we were looking for, the device was then detonated and both were blown up – the bomb and the ground mine.

If that procedure didn't work, we would have a plan B – on one occasion this involved using a piece of old fire hose, packing plastic explosive into it, diving down to the ground mine and wrapping the snake-like device around it, setting a timer and blowing it up that way. Most of the mines, of course, had been floating about since WWII. One of the main places we used to find these old wartime mines was down by the Isle of Arran. I don't know why, but even to this day there are still a lot of explosive devices found down there. Around the Western Isles was another area where there were more than you would expect – although we tackled the majority of these west coast ones during my later service at the Faslane base, rather than on the minehunter.

However, it was during my time on HMS Kedleston that I gained a lot of vital experience and learned the bulk of my trade although I had a lot of fun on jollies as well. We went across to Norway and spent a couple of days there for the Norwegian Independence Day and we had an extraordinarily good time. Keep reading and I'll tell you about who I met there – including a footballing celebrity. Once I had finished my year on HMS Kedlestone in 1973, I was told I was going to be sent to a diving team. "Murray, you are going to HMS Neptune."

What? What kind of boat is that? I soon learned that Faslane was a big submarine base near Helensburgh, officially known in navyspeak as HMS Neptune. There were quite a number of guys making up the Faslane Diving Team and it took a while to get to know them all, and to find out just what our duties were going to be in the team. A lot of hard work was involved with those boats. We never called them submarines or even subs, although I will here, as I suspect most of the readers of this fine volume will in fact be scruffy civilian types.

We had the nuclear Polaris subs on our doorstep and we had a floating dock just a short distance away – AFD60, the Admiralty Floating Dock – a massive structure. It was in constant use, with subs slipping in and out, and our duties involved setting up the blocks for them to rest on when the water was pumped out of the dock, and connecting the cooling hoses for the nuclear reactors inside the subs. Then, when the sub was flooded again we had to disconnect all these hoses. Alongside the jetty, there was always underwater work to be done. This included changing the propellers on the older, smaller diesel subs – and also on the larger Polaris ones like HMS Resolution, Repulse or Renown. There was a lot of heavy work involved in that. The propellers on those big boys weighed about 21 tons and it meant working with cranes and the tides. It was all about getting the weight exactly right on the stern of the submarine and on the crane. We worked our guts out, setting up massive hydraulic extracting gear called pilgrim nuts, to break the seal and get the propeller off. That could take hours or even days.

There were huge lifting lugs which we screwed into the top of the propeller and I remember one day we were in the process of taking a massive prop off, using a dockside crane, when one snapped with a crack which I can only describe as like a rifle shot.

To tell the truth, I was very lucky to be alive because if that propeller had fallen on top of me I wouldn't be here now. That, or the whiplash of the steel wire rope, so close that I could hear and feel the pressure wave as the cold steel sliced through the water just inches away, could have cut me in half. The gods were with me that day and I escaped injury with not even a scratch and surfaced just a little shaken, much to the relief of the surface team.

Before the propeller came off we had a great big boss nut at the end of the shaft which in itself weighed tons and had a huge thread. The divers were stuck for a long time trying to remove it and although we fitted purchase levers to it we didn't have enough muscle to unscrew the thing. It was very awkward and lots of people, including the commanding officer himself, were saying "We'll do it this way," and "We'll do it that way," but these guys weren't under the water like we were. It was all very well shouting from the surface but it just wasn't going to work.

When I went down to have a look, I thought, 'I'll get right down to about 15 feet below, put air into my suit and I'll shoot straight up towards the surface, aim myself for that lever bar and hit it with my shoulder. It might move or I might end up with an injury. Worth a try.'

I began the swim up to the surface, building up speed then, wallop. I hit the steel lever bar hard with my shoulder.

Ouch. Jesus, that was sore but, hey, I felt it move. Unscrewing the boss nut was a long, slow process. I was down there until night fell, along with another diver by the name of Doby Lines, before I even got a few turns off. It was a case of having to swim really hard to move that lever even a little bit. When I completed the dive, the Chief Diver shouted, "What's happening down there? You've been there all this time and there's bugger-all happening."

"Actually, chief," I said, "that's the boss nut about a quarter way off so you can send down a fresh pair of divers to finish the job."

His eyes narrowed as he looked at me and said, "How the hell did you do that?" When I explained to him what I had done, he just laughed and said, "Christ, King Kong."

That was it. My name was KK for the rest of my time with the Faslane Diving Team. Actually, I was quite pleased with myself for getting that tricky one done on my own just using a bit of brainpower and shoulder power to get the job done.

We used to have to do full checks of the submarines when they came back from abroad. They might have gone all over the world, perhaps for six months or a year, and we had to give them a full body check. Obviously, some scrapes here or there might be found and endless reports had to be submitted to the powers-that-be about their condition. They were always anxious about the windows at the bow of the submarine (not glass by the way). These windows were something to do with the sonar equipment and could sometimes be in a poor state when the subs came back in.

One particular time I had taken photos and completed my report when I was called into an office by a high-ranking officer. He asked me what I had actually seen at the bow of the submarine. I explained to him what I found during the inspection. He said I was to mention nothing to anyone else. "Nothing. Not even to your commanding officer." I was sworn to secrecy.

Later, when I was in the AFD60 floating dock, I was checking over another sub. You can't check them over in five minutes – it can take a long time to swim from one end to the other. The boss said, "Can you check the propeller when you're down there?"

When I got to the back end I didn't find the propeller but I did find what looked like a cage with a huge fan inside it. I had never seen anything like it and obviously I couldn't check it because I couldn't get at it.

When I surfaced, I made my report to the Chief Diver. I said "Chief, there's no propeller on that submarine."

He looked at me and said, "Chris, what the hell have you been on? Are you telling me there's no propeller on it?"

"Yes, chief. There's something inside a big cage."

"Away you go," he said.

Huh, don't believe me, then! However, I also reported what I had seen to the CO and I think he too, thought I was on the wacky baccy. They then obviously had a discussion between themselves and once again, I was hauled up to the office in front of the HRO. That's a high-ranking officer, for all you landlubbers. After I told him what I had seen, he whispered, "Diver Murray, what you think you saw down there, you never saw at all, did you?"

Latching on smartish, I replied, "No, I never saw anything at all." That was the right answer as far as he was concerned.

In truth, I found all the subterfuge quite amusing. It was a fan of some sort that was powering the sub. There were blades inside there; it certainly wasn't the normal kind of propeller. It was a new sort of propulsion system for submarines which they were apparently testing but officially nobody knew anything about it. I imagine it was to make the subs quieter because every propeller has its own identity. Each has its own distinctive sound which was why we changed propellers so often at Faslane. Probably to confuse the Russians who knew exactly which submarine was which by the sound of the propeller.

They still knew that you were there but they didn't know which submarine it was. I think these secret fans were tried out as a quieter method of propulsion. That's what I concluded anyway, although I never did see official confirmation of it.

We also spent time at Faslane working on anti-swimming devices in case anybody tried to get into the base by swimming or diving. There were lots of devices set under the water, and on the surface, for this purpose. One of the main tasks of the duty diver was to patrol the jetties before the nuclear submarines sailed and, when no one was looking, to accidentally knock over, into the water, a couple of kegs of beer which would be lined up, ready to be loaded on board. Later, when all was quiet, these kegs would be recovered from their watery beer store and transported to our small bar in the diving unit.

Only half of our diving team would be working on the submarines. Normally, the other half were away on the diving boat, Yo-Yo, or away on what we called the milk run, which was ordnance disposal at the request of police or coastguards in places like the Western Isles, Orkney and Shetland. Someone might report an explosive device somewhere and the team's job was to go round and clear these devices away, whether they be mines, mortar bombs or whatever. People find these things from time to time on beaches, in their gardens and even sometimes in their lofts. The team members would go round, carefully collect these devices and take them to a safe area and blow them up. Sometimes suspicious-looking packages or envelopes would turn up at various locations and they had to be dealt with carefully in case they turned out to be parcel bombs or IEDs (improvised explosive devices).

As well as disposing of all such potentially hazardous devices it was also standard practice, after completing the job, to visit as many pubs as we could. It was like part of the job, really, although I don't think I ever found the advice 'Now go to the pub' in the operations manual. We'd be staying in hotels and were being paid subsistence so we always had a bit of money in our pockets. We worked hard and played hard. One of the places we used to regularly visit was Rothesay on the Isle of Bute. We often did deep diving round there. Faslane had the only diving team in Britain at that time with the capability to dive to 250 feet on air. It was done on surface demand diving equipment, with hoses supplying air to the diver and banks of air bottles, oxygen, decompression chambers and so on. We were trained to dive to that depth simply because at some point there may have been an urgent military or emergency requirement to do so.

We trained for a range of scenarios. For example, a sub might have a serious mechanical problem which had caused it to lie on the sea bed. Firstly, we would have to get air into the sub to keep the crew alive. For that, we had a device called the Cox's Gun which was a massive piece of equipment and very heavy. It was capable of firing bolts through the pressure hull of a submarine with hoses connected which would inject air into the sub. That Cox's Gun, and other rescue equipment which we might have to use, was set in containers outside the diving store in Faslane. It was called Submiss gear.

There were different categories of alert: if a submarine went down for whatever reason and couldn't get back to the surface that was a Submiss, the first alert. The next stage was Subsmash and the third was Subsunk, when it was confirmed that a sub was actually on the bottom and needed rescuing. Although we were at constant readiness, no call ever came while I was there. Since my days everything has been upgraded so much that I doubt if that rescue equipment is still there. We had to be ready for any sort of thing, from salvage to body recovery. It's what we were trained for. It's no job for the faint-hearted because you can be expected to do some really gruesome stuff.

The town of Stornoway on the Isle of Lewis, my current home, was one of the places our team used to go to regularly to blow up ordnance that had been found. Sometimes on our visits the police might ask us to do something for them since we were on the island. More than once a trip ended with a search for the body of someone who had gone over the pier. It wasn't a very nice part of the job but it was a vital service. There was also the huge satisfaction when you found the remains and could return them to the family. I do remember on one occasion, after a big night out, we were called by police to search for a missing fisherman in Stornoway harbour.

On our arrival, it was plain to see the water in the harbour was yucky and very dark. Having sunk a few the night before, body recovery wasn't an ideal task for clearing the head. However, we got a team of divers sorted out and descended into the murkiness. Even with high-powered torches, it was difficult to see anything on the seabed. At one point, a diver working near to me saw the light from my torch and decided to give me a fright by coming from behind and pouncing onto my back as I searched. It gave me a fright alright. I nearly had a hairy fit, in fact. Thank you, Garry Macleod . . . I have never forgiven you for that one. Shortly after that, and just after bumping into a shopping trolley, I felt what I thought was a shoe. It was, and a leg was attached. Instinctively, I pulled the leg, causing the body to rise up towards me, and I found myself looking straight at the white, ghost-like face of the deceased. A scary moment.

Apart from the explosives ordnance disposal around the West Coast, there were also lighter times when we would go down to Ardfern in West Argyll. We used to know the people quite well in a place called Galley of Lorne Hotel, I don't know if it's still called that. The hotel was owned, I think, by the Laird of Lunga, one Colin Macdougall. A very tall handsome chap, with a big earring in his left ear and long hair, he had a great sense of humour. We had some good times there and as well as EOD we would dive for scallops around the Loch Melfort and Corryvreckan areas. Occasionally we would come back with a bag or two of clams and Colin, the laird, would ask for some. In return, we would be invited round to his huge house.

The massive banquet table would be laid out, set with all sorts of wines and spirits. After a feed of clams and the usual banter at the banquet table, Colin usually suggested a game of Murder. Oo-er, this was the first place I ever heard the term 'murder' for a game – and in such a spooky environment as a castle. The first time I encountered this game I was with some guys who had played it before and it was a game that involved each and every one of us, including the staff of the castle and hotel. The game normally went on for most of the night. Just like you see on the TV programme *Miss Marple*, someone would be 'killed' and we would try and find the murderer. The idea was to work through the suspects but it was a lot more fun than that. There were so many rooms in this castle and lots of boltholes and, as there were a lot of guys and girls much about the same age in this place, (Colin employed some very good-looking girls from north and south of the border), it was a great excuse to have a good old time – if you know what I mean . . . That's what it was really all about; never mind your Murder game.

I remember an occasion we were down at West Loch, Tarbert, in Argyll and doing some diving work. It was my birthday and that night we had a fine old time. The whole diving team and the guys and girls from the Victoria Hotel in Tarbert were there. The next morning we decided to head back to Ardfern to do some diving. I was down at about 100 feet and I started to feel really unwell, with a growing pain in my abdomen. Now, I know the difference between the after-effects of a boozy session and when there is something seriously wrong with me. It was more than just a hangover. I had dived in that condition before, as most of the lads had, but on this occasion it was much more serious. I was at depth, shivering and about to throw up, knowing if I did that I might choke or even drown. That sort of thing is bad enough even in your home environment but at the bottom of the sea, with a fair tide running, it's a bit more challenging. Trying to remain calm and slowly head to the surface with my heart racing and about to pass out, was difficult, whilst also understanding that if I did not control my ascent I was at risk of getting an embolism, or the bends. Sickening it definitely was.

I really felt more dead than alive and had begun to vomit although I managed to flush out my mask and, just as importantly, vent off the air in my suit. It seemed a very long way to the surface. I knew it was going to be touch and go, and if I was to make it I had to stay conscious. Seconds ticked by and I surfaced but must have passed out. The next thing I knew, I was being dragged into the dive boat and the guys were checking to make sure I was in the land of the living. I was taken back to my hotel room where I began to vomit again. Oh, how they laughed. Saying I couldn't handle my drink, they took the mickey. Yet I was pleading for help because I didn't know what was wrong with me.

Fortunately, the local postmistress, Kirsty, a lovely lady, was in the hotel and did a couple of tests. She was also the local nurse and she told one of the officers to find a Land Rover and get me down to Lochgilphead immediately, for onward transit in an ambulance to the Vale of Leven Hospital. All of a sudden the mood changed. The team realised that there was something seriously wrong with me. I had appendicitis and I was in a really bad way. Off we went, and I think one of the scariest moments I have ever had in my life was in the front seat of that Land Rover with the driver, by the name of Lawrie Lawrence, doing 100 miles per hour all the way down to Lochgilphead. An ambulance then took me on another fast drive to the Vale of Leven

Hospital. Straight into the operating theatre, I was operated on right away. Just in time. Any longer and my appendix would have burst. Close shaves? I've had a few.

The navy was proud of its diving teams; a rough, tough bunch of characters but, at the same time, part of the elite of the Royal Navy. Joe Public was welcome to come onto the base and have a look round our kit and stores and have one of us explain to them what the diving teams were about. There were always one or two people who volunteered to show these people around, whether they be school-kids or students or whoever. They were shown what equipment we used, why we used it, where we used it, when we used it and what was involved in the work of the diving teams, whether it be explosives, working with submarines or whatever. It was always patiently explained and people were invited to ask questions. It was satisfying, explaining to the public what diving was all about because most people knew nothing whatsoever about it.

Royal Navy diving is different to most other kinds of diving. We had diving teams going to various parts of Northern Scotland, including the Crinan Canal, Scrabster, Orkney and we used to perform diving displays. You might wonder how we could have diving displays when diving is done underwater, but we used to do high-speed surface displays and fast boat pickups. That was exciting for the public. A fast boat zooming along with one of the diving team at the front, holding a strop over the side, and a diver punching his arm into it and being ripped into the boat at full speed. To an amateur, it looks as if the move is going to take the diver's arm off but actually, with the momentum of the boat and the diver being in water, the high-speed manoeuvre would just flip him into the boat. Things could still go wrong, however. If the diver in the water chickened out halfway through, it could rip his flipping arm off. That sort of dramatic activity, with flares and thunder flashes going off all over the place, as a bunch of hairy-assed divers did silly things in the water for public entertainment, was fun to watch. It was for us too.

One stunt we often did at the start of any display was the 'flaming arseholes' trick. That's what we called it. One of the divers, and to be honest it was always me, would be dressed up in an old drysuit with a hood over the head and become the star of a particularly spectacular show. At the end of a high pier, sometimes on a motorbike, or just a bicycle, or even under my own steam, I would race along the length of the pier. The diving officer would say over the public address system something like: "This is Diver Murray. This is what we do to a diver who doesn't stand his hand in the pub when he's supposed to." There I would be, putting my hands up in the air and shaking my head, and a guy would come along with a couple of gallons of petrol, pour it over me and then set me alight. This caused a huge fireball and that was the time to start running.

Some advice from someone who has been there. The most important thing to remember when you have been turned into a ball of flame is to keep calm and have a wee think about what you are going to do next. Timing is important. You have to make sure that you don't slip, for instance. In my case, I would run along the pier, a dodgy tactic too, because once you start moving you can't stop or you could be engulfed by the flames. I would only have a matter of a few yards to go before I leapt off the pier with the flames still behind me as I hit the water with a big splash. I do remember once trying to cycle off the end of a pier and my boots were so slippery with petrol on the rubber pedals that they just kept slipping off. That time I fell in a heap in a big fireball and the other guys more or less kicked me off the pier like a rag doll. Oh, how they laughed . . . again. The spectators thought it was just part of the show and cheered loudly as I lay there feeling a frighteningly ferocious heat that was about to burn through my suit and roast my ass.

That kind of mishap did happen more than once – which was why we stopped using the bikes and just had a running jump at it. There were no health and safety issues or risk assessments like they have nowadays. We did what we wanted and we usually got away with it. We were the only section of the Royal Navy at that time who could get away with bending the rules – and it was great fun. After jumping into the water and coming back out again when the flames were extinguished, a young lady would invariably come along with a drink from the beer tent. There could be a Guinness tent there or, if we were really lucky, perhaps a whisky tent. These were community gala days and someone would always bring a drink to the still-damp star of the show. With all the new rules about health and safety those kinds of displays never happen nowadays. I used to enjoy doing that type of thing.

After the display was finished we would get into party mode again unless, of course, we were called away to deal with bombs or mines found somewhere else. The social life on the Faslane base was fast and varied for those who were based there. Under normal circumstances, if there wasn't any work to be done on the submarines, we would usually finish work about 5pm, go back to the billet and get dobied, another term for washed, and head off to the pubs on the base. We had a couple of bars there: one was the Trident Club and the other was the skittle alley. And there was yet another bar, where the submariners would meet, way down in the basement, naturally.

We would all keep to our own bars. The guys who went to the skittle alley, for example, liked music, and lots of bands played there. There was also fierce competition between the submariners and the rest of us. The submariners called the people who worked on surface ships 'skimmers'. The skimmers, meanwhile, called the submariners 'diesel weasels'. Us divers were 'bubbleheads'. A lot of banter went on and after a few drinks there would be singing, shouting and now and again a bit of trouble would start. A submariner would always get obnoxious about who they were and what they were. They didn't like bubbleheads and they didn't like skimmers because they were submariners. So it was inevitable we would come to blows sometimes. We ended up with black eyes, bloody noses, chipped teeth and goodness knows what else.

The survivors would appear back in the diving store the following morning and we would discover who had been scrapping with who. There would then be another battle royale when we met again the following weekend.

We had quite a lot of lovely Wrens on base too. They would also get involved in the fights sometimes, and some of them were better at scrapping than the lads. There were a few thousand of us on the base at that time – Royal Marines, Wrens, submariners, civilian workers and the many military police based there.

I remember being on duty one night when a PO diver called Scouse Lewis asked me if I would get the bomb disposal Land Rover, go to Garelochhead and meet another diving team from down south. I was to pick up a package and take it back to base.

"Don't bother asking about the package, just take it back to the base," he said. I refused because I wanted to know exactly what was in this package before I would take responsibility for it. At that time we had Marines on the gate and they checked every vehicle going in and out, for explosive devices. I didn't want to be caught with something dodgy when I didn't know even know what it was. Eventually he told me it was two cases of scrumpy cider. 'Ah, well,' I thought, 'OK. I'll take it back.' I'd never tasted scrumpy before and I'd go and get it as long as I got a pint for myself.

"You're more than welcome, son," he said.

Off I went to Garelochhead with the usual wave from the Marines, brandishing their rifles on the security gate. I met with two guys; one was a Chief and one was a PO, and they handed the package over. Thankfully, I was waved through security with the cases of scrumpy hidden under some diving bottles at the back of the Land Rover. I took them up to the mess – two big cardboard boxes with taps on them and Scouse said, "Next Friday night, you come over to my mess and you'll get a pint of this." Great. I really wanted to sample this famous cider stuff but it was going to be my downfall, although I didn't know that at the time.

Off I went on the Friday night, all dressed up to the nines and ready to go out on the base. Scouse Lewis, the PO Diver, was a seasoned drinker who knew all about scrumpy and had been drinking it for years. I went up to his mess and he opened up his wardrobe and took out a glass. When he opened the wardrobe, the stink was almost unbearable and the glass he took out had mould hanging off it. I felt sick as soon as I saw it and desperately hoped he wasn't going to give me anything out of that manky glass. He was.

Sensing my disgust, he said, "A proper cider drinker never washes his glass." I don't know where this came from but it really sickened me. However, being a rough, tough CD I knew I couldn't back out. I took my first mouthful and almost threw up straightaway. It was that bloody awful. For some reason I had expected it to be something smooth like apple juice. No. Scrumpy is lumpy. There could have been anything in that foul concoction – dead cats, judging by the stench. Determined not to be a Highlander who's branded a wuss, I steeled myself and struggled my way through a pint of it. Then Scouse said perkily, "Another pint, Chris?"

"Er, no thanks. I can't take any more of that stuff," I mumbled, as he poured another pint down his neck in a oner.

"Right. We're going down to the skittle alley now."

We got down there and he ordered two large Wood's. No, we were not tucking into planks. Wood's is demerara rum. You will know it. It's the one with 'Old Navy Rum' on the label. And it's really strong. I got the first one down but as I ordered the second round, I had to sprint to the door. I just made it to the toilet and was sick. Very, very, disgustingly sick, in a foul-smelling splish-splosh kind of 'now-I-am-going-to-have-to-wipe-down-the-pan-and-the-cistern' kind of way. I felt really good. Brand new. Yaay! I was ready to resume drinking operations. And then I was sick again.

As I ran for the door, Scouse was laughing and shouting, "Chris, you'll never make a good cider drinker at all."

It must take years of practise to drink that stuff properly and not get sick, and I'm afraid trying to do that in one night was an impossibility for one as well brought up as myself. He was right about one thing, though. I never made it as a cider drinker. In fact, I never touched cider again, and I don't think I ever touched Wood's Rum either for the rest of my puff. Yeuch. That was an experience I am happy to forget.

CHAPTER 3

As members of the Faslane diving team CD3 – that's Clearance Diving Team 3 – one of the jobs we trained for was to become attack swimmers. Our main job, apart from base work, was EOD or explosive ordnance disposal, but as attack swimmers we were also taught how to place limpet mines on ships. Exercises were arranged to allow us to practise these attacks. One day, I think it might have been off Ettrick Bay on the island of Bute, on our diving boat, the Yo-Yo, we were dressed up in our black wetsuits, with our black re-breathing oxygen sets on, masks and fins too, ready for anything. The idea was to swim from our boat to a ship in the distance. Just so you get the picture, this was in the middle of the night with a heavy sea and snow storms. We had to battle through all that weather, all the while having to work on compass readings. We could only just see the ship lights in the distance.

Our task was to swim out to her with an imitation limpet mine. It took a long time getting out the mile or so to the ship, but we were elite attack swimmers and we were expected to do this without any moans and groans. We just had to bloody well get on with it. We'd surface swim out until we reached a certain range from the target. Then on went the masks, we'd swim down just beneath the surface of the water and place the mine on the hull. We then had to surface and be taken aboard by the security crew on board. As if the evening hadn't been thrilling enough, we were then 'arrested'. Thrown into the cells aboard the ship, we were closely interrogated; name, rank and number was all we were allowed to give. From there, we were carted off, back to

Faslane, and thrown into the cells for a couple of days. Very realistic.

All this time, we would be closely questioned by charming MPs (military police officers), all kitted out with a beautiful sense of sarcasm and, to make these close encounters especially enjoyable, the obligatory stinky breath. Bet they chewed cloves of garlic beforehand. And that was just a normal couple of days work for us divers. There were six or seven of us aboard the Yo-Yo, with two of us going to the ship each time. One to port, one to starboard. That was the dreaded attack swimming and we just had to get on with it. We had to undertake these exercises on a regular basis to keep our skills honed, and if there were any cock-ups we would be pretty severely reprimanded. We wouldn't make the same mistakes twice. For example, coming too close to the ship and being spotted by the search parties on board before we dived down.

We were all on our tod. It was dark; it was cold and, ach, what was the point of moaning? There was no one to hold our hands, to say 'good job' or to tell us not to worry. The philosophy was simple – you are an attack swimmer so do it all yourself. We had to use our heads and do what we thought was right, exactly as we were trained to. If we didn't, we were in big soapy bubble.

Once, the crew of my ship, HMS Kedleston, went up a fjord in Norway to a place called Drammen for a courtesy visit. I think we got there on Norwegian Independence Day. That was fun. Bands were playing and I remember when we went ashore we had to wear our uniforms. There was a sacred tree, for reasons that I don't quite recall now, in the middle of the square. A couple of the boys climbed it and got into monumental trouble with the authorities. In fact, quite a few of us got into bother on that trip. On the first day, we found a bar called the Cutty Sark. The strange thing about this bar was that they had great big burly bouncers on the door and a very unusual door policy. We could get as drunk as we wanted: no matter how steaming we got, nobody bothered with us, but as soon as someone fell asleep, they were promptly flung outside.

You'd have thought that at least if you were asleep, you were quiet. No, you were summarily ejected. Two of our guys got thrown out as the afternoon session wore on – no, I wasn't one of them. With my growing interest in photography, I was busy taking pictures of the bouncers hurling my mates out in the street. Well, couldn't miss an action shot. After a couple of hours, we began to realise just how extremely expensive the beer was. Extortionate it was.

Some of the locals made their own hooch and they had different flavourings. I found this out to my cost one night when we went on to a place outside the town called the Brackens Hall for a wee dance. One of the Norwegian boys produced a bottle of some homemade stuff and handed it to me. I put it to my lips and took a good swallow but he grabbed the bottle before I could take any more.

He protested, "No, no, no you don't take that much." It was only then that I twigged it was neat alcohol, with no flavouring whatsoever. Really horrible to taste, it burned all the way down. Yes, I was violently sick outside. Probably just as well, otherwise it might have permanently damaged my insides. Still, we were in Drammen for three days so there was plenty of time to check out the local culture – their get-togethers were a bit like our ceilidhs, with wine, women and song.

With our ship alongside, the only respite our livers got from partying was when it was our turn for duty. Someone had to make sure no one got up the gangway that wasn't supposed to. These spells on duty – the dogwatches – were a couple of hours here and there. It was just a case of looking after the ship, checking the ropes and making sure everything was fine. We did our duties and then when we were finished, we were away ashore again, catching up with the rest of the lads and having a jolly time on shore.

The coxswain on board was Nobby Clark from Edinburgh who served as Chief Diver and, I have to say, he was a fair man who went out of his way to help anyone at any time, at sea or on shore. When we left Drammen we organised a clay pigeon shoot on board the ship; the cox had an over-and-under shotgun and I had a semi-automatic one. At that time, the Navy allowed ratings to carry weapons on the ship. I won, of course. The prize was a bottle of Southern Comfort. Not a good idea because I somehow became the worse for wear and was put into the aft end of the ship, out of everybody's way, until my head cleared.

We arrived back in the UK and headed for Port Edgar, close to the Forth Bridge – now a yachting marina – where the minehunting crews always met up for a jar or six. Most of these ships had their own dog on board at that time. Ours was called Sparkle. It wasn't a very nice thing to do, but back then we used to meet up in the pub and all the dogs would come with us too. These sea dogs weren't thrown snacks like crisps, as often happens in a bar. No, these bow-wows would be given beer just like the rest of the Jolly Jack Tars. Competitions were held to see whose dog would last the longest without collapsing and flopping, sprawled out on all fours. It sounds rather cruel but it was part of the entertainment. Oh, and in case you're wondering, I am told that particular tradition doesn't happen at all anymore.

The worst seas I've seen were while I was on the Kedleston in the Pentland Firth. She was a wooden minehunter, although I believe now they are built largely from some type of plastic. Being so light, these boats really were like a cork on the ocean and one day, coming through the firth, we hit some serious weather with dreadful sea conditions. There were half a dozen of us on the bridge when we hit this lump of water. Well, it was like we were climbing up the side of a house. The ship went down the other side of the wave and keeled over about 45 degrees. Everyone on the bridge was thrown against the bulkheads or onto the deck of the wheelhouse.

Three or four of the guys were injured, one quite badly. Others had fractured fingers and bruising. There was a lot of damage above and below decks. It was one of these things that you do experience in the navy and was especially true of a light minehunter like HMS Kedleston. We experienced rough seas coming back from Norway too, but never as bad as the Pentland Firth. It was certainly a lesson to me on how small we humans are, and how very big and powerful the ocean can be.

While we were on exercise on Arran we were asked to move a Second World War bunker to preserve a landmark beside it. This was a Viking stone which was only a matter of a couple of yards away from an old concrete bunker. We were asked by the local authorities to blow up this bunker to get rid of it – but, and this was the important bit, without damaging the ancient stone. We had to fill sandbags on the shore – a long way below the bunker – hump them up the hill, and place them around the stone to protect it.

A heck of a lot of sandbags were involved. Do you know how much a bag of sand weighs? A lot. That was a job which took its toll on everybody; going back and fore from the beach all day, with the Chief Petty Officer screaming at us to get it done smartish. Explosive charges were then laid in the old bunker. By the time we had placed the last sack on top of the stone, it was getting close to detonation time. Once all the bags were in place we had to clear the area to make sure there were no civilians anywhere near the zone, which we had red-flagged to make sure no one could get caught in the blast. The detonation went well. Boom. The old bunker was flattened in a second or two and when the dust cleared, the landmark stone was still standing proud. It remains there, standing proudly on that hill, to this day. A job well done, but a lot of really hard graft involved to preserve that stone whilst demolishing the ugly concrete building beside it. As dusk fell, we retired to an Arran hostelry. This was not recreation, of course. No, no, this was vital training – discussing the detonation and the finer points of filling sandbags.

Passions and tempers sometimes got the better of some of the guys on the team. One of the commanding officers even got involved in a bit of a fracas with one of the lower ranks in the diving team. The diver was George Nelson. George, a fantastic guy from the Newcastle area, liked his grog, as we all did. It was on a diving exercise, somewhere off the Kyles of Bute, that tempers got a bit frayed and I saw the results of all this when the guys came back to base. Little George had a stonker of a black eye and a burst lip. I decided against asking him what had happened. Sometimes it's better to keep one's tongue in check. I found out later that the two of them had come to blows, which should never happen between a commanding officer and a low-ranking diver.

The whole diving exercise was aborted and we never did find out what was actually said but after that, when any dirty job came up, it was poor old George the Pig who was sent. A blocked sewer? Right, send George. Funnily enough, he was content enough with these awful, smelly jobs. Like a pig in s**t, we would say. That particular lieutenant commander had a pretty severe temper himself so he may have been at fault. I believe he came through the ranks and wasn't the most subtle of men. Happily, I never had the distinction of walloping my commanding officer, or vice versa. I did have a ruck with a Chief Diver once or twice, but that was as high up the chain of command that I went.

My ship, HMS Kedleston, was in Dover when we received orders to pay a courtesy visit to Boulogne. I had never been to France so that was a good one for me. When we arrived we were told if we went ashore we would have to wear our number ones, our special occasion uniform. These were captain's orders and we were none too happy. We didn't want to stand out – we wanted to boogie. Off we went in a wee group and disappeared into Boulogne. After visiting a few watering holes, very unlike the bars we were used to in Portsmouth, me, Barney Brett and a third fellow found ourselves in a friendly little tavern. I noticed the barmaid was a stunning-looking woman and I suppose after a few drinks, dim lights, soft music, I thought I'd fallen in love.

It was just one of those wonderful evenings. I remember sauntering across to the jukebox which was playing a memorably fine tune, *Ballad of Death Valley*. A haunting, whistling tune which I recently rediscovered when a friend found it on YouTube. It was a hit back then, in 1972, for the German performer Peter Henn. I got talking to the barmaid when I went up for drinks, She had a little English and I was whispering sweet nothings in her ear. By this stage it was pretty much gibberish, but she was responding to the banter and took one or two drinks herself. The atmosphere was very sultry. Ah, there was romance in the air as far as I was concerned. Things started getting a wee bit hotter between me and this lass as she showed me round her charming pub.

More songs were put on the jukebox and we headed off to another room where we kissed and canoodled. Unknown to me, a man then came into the bar looking for her. He was getting quite loudly upset that he couldn't find her. Boyfriend or husband, this was her man. After a while the two of us returned to the bar, with the romantic strains of *Ballad of Death Valley* playing again on the jukebox as we entered. Suddenly, this guy appeared out of nowhere, screaming and shouting, brandishing what I soon deduced was a rather large shotgun. Rather worryingly, I also quickly realised he was pointing it straight at me. Right then, everybody else started screaming and I thought, 'This isn't real. This can't be happening.'

My mate, Barney Brett, leapt across the room and began to remonstrate with the aggressive Frenchman, trying to snatch the gun away from him. However, the unhappy Frenchman was stronger than he looked and pulled the shotgun back and pointed it straight at Barney. In the melee that followed, the gun began to swing back towards me but, as the excitable gentleman turned, I caught the barrel and pushed it up towards the ceiling. Next thing – boomph!

It went off, blowing an almighty hole in the ceiling. Bits of plaster rained down into the wines and les biéres on the tables. People began to scream and run out of the bar. It was like watching something out of a movie; just as unreal. All throughout the commotion, that incredible haunting tune, *Ballad of Death Valley*, was still playing loudly on the jukebox. It may seem funny, looking back on it now, but it was pretty serious being there at the time.

After the shot was fired, I figured there were no more rounds in the gun and the danger was over. Barney, however, was taking no chances. He shouted, "Come on Chris, let's get bloody out of here."

We legged it out the door. The pretty barmaid had somehow vanished but I wasn't going to ask if anyone had seen her. Galloping down the road, Barney said, "Don't stop. Don't look round. Just keep on running."

Just then, there was another loud cracking sound. Something with the force of a flying brick thumped into my leg and back and I went down in a heap on the cobbles. There was no pain but there was a lot of blood spattered about. It slowly dawned on me that I had been shot. Sorry, but I hadn't been shot before so I didn't know what it felt like. Bang. Thump. Blood. Aaargh.

Barney pulled me in under a window and another bullet ricocheted off the windowsill. This time Barney was hit by the blast. The angry chap at the bar was reloading and he was out for the kill. Then, just like in the best movies, a police car drove up and the crazed gunman fled back into the bar. Unfortunately, the two cops in the car must have been the two doziest gendarmes in the whole of France. They saw me lying there in my crumpled number one sailor's uniform. Maybe they didn't notice the rivers of blood oozing from my broken body into the gutter. They just drove past. What were they thinking? Probably, "Ee-haw, ee-haw. Another of zeez drunken Breeteesh sailors. Vat are zey like, Jean Pierre?"

We couldn't believe it. Fearful that the gun-toting maniac would return at any time, Barney continued to drag me further down the road, as far away as possible from the Jealousy Inn. We spotted an ambulance and Barney tried to wave it down. They, too, just looked at us and kept going as though they wanted nothing to do with us. By then, I could feel the blood trickling down my left leg and into my shoes. Why was my backside so wet? Oh, no! I realised I had been shot in the bum as well. Still unsure where else I had been punctured, I could see blood on my hand and I just didn't know what kind of condition I was in.

We had to get to a hospital somehow but nobody would come near us. They just didn't want to know. I was still being dragged along by Barney when we came across a posh hotel with a couple of flunkeys standing outside. We were desperate. Barney pushed one of them aside and threatened the other one to help us. He helped me into the plush foyer. Of course, first chance they got, they called the gendarmes. The real reason for summoning the law was that they didn't want riff-raff like us leaking crimson stuff over their expensive carpets. When the officers arrived, an ambulance was called and at last I was wheeled off to hospital. I was conscious until we got there.

When I came round in the morning I was in a lot of pain. I had been shot in the backside, in my left leg and in my left arm. The nurses cleaned me up and I remember one coming up with a big smile on her face as she produced this huge syringe, with a giant needle at the end of it. I was made to bend over the side of the bed and this needle was injected, nay hammered, into my bum. Not surprisingly, I passed out again. Coming to, the same nurse was looking over me, again with a big smile on her face. I suspect she got a lot of satisfaction shoving that needle into the Murray posterior.

Seemingly, during the night I had been calling her 'cherie d'amour' and I don't think she had appreciated that, coming from a dribbling, drunken sailor as it did. An interpreter was eventually summoned and a detective came to see me. He informed me I had been shot by a combination machine, a cross between a shotgun and a rifle, and I had a bullet lodged in my left leg as well as shotgun pellets in my backside and left arm. My injuries would require medication for some time to counteract any damage that may have been done to my muscles, and to stop any poisonous substances coursing through my body. I gave them a statement and soon afterwards, I was taken back to HMS Kedleston and speedily taken back across the channel to the Buckland Hospital in Dover. However, much as I appreciate the work of the National Health Service, I have to say that one or two mistakes were made there, at Dover Hospital.

Staff had to take x-rays of the bullet lodged in my leg so they strapped a nail file onto my leg, with the point of the nail file placed at the bullet entry point, as a point of reference. Luckily, the bullet had missed the bone and was lodged in the muscle. I was then taken to the Canterbury Accident Unit where a surgeon looked over his glasses at me in a very serious way and told me he'd never seen the like in his life. He wanted to know what kind of gun I was shot with.

"Was it a blunderbuss?"

"It didn't look like a blunderbuss," I said.

"Well, whatever it was, it fired a lot of big stuff – some of it from his girl's handbag by the looks of it. There's actually a nail file jammed inside your leg, as well as the bullet."

"What?"

"Yes," he said. "Have a look at the x-rays. You can see the nail file in your leg."

That's when I started laughing. This baffled him even more. When I told him the nail file had actually been strapped to my leg, to pinpoint where the bullet was, his chin dropped and he howled with laughter. He apologised, whispering, "I'm very sorry, Mr Murray, but this information was not passed to me at all."

It was an embarrassing episode for me. Word had spread around the navy about what had happened to muggins and to Barney. He'd taken a few shotgun pellets in his arm and his leg but his wounds were superficial. Some of the newspapers around Portsmouth heard about it but they never got the full details.

My next hospital stop-off was HMS Hasler in Portsmouth. While I thought the bullet would be removed, the experts decided it would be too dangerous as the extraction might severely damage my leg muscle. It was safer for the bullet to remain where it was. As for the shotgun pellets, a lot of them are also still in me although some were plucked out by the nurses in France. How long will it take before I am poisoned by this lump of lead in me? Who knows? I still think about this because the main bullet is still there and there are shotgun pellets still lodged in my buttocks. Sorry, I realise you may not have been expecting such detailed medical information. For some strange reason, the alarm goes off more often when I go through an airport scanner than it did before. Can't think why.

When I was reunited with the ship's crew in Port Edgar, it took quite a long time for me to live down the incident in France. They wouldn't leave it alone. That was a hassle, especially as I didn't want my father, back in Dornoch, to hear what had happened to me. The next time I went home on leave, I thought it best not to mention anything at all. Until one night, we were sat by the fire and Dad asked, "So how's your leg and your backside, by the way? You've got to remember you've got a brother in the Royal Navy who hears everything that's going on." He hooted with laughter and added, "I'm glad you're OK but just be very careful that the women you choose are unattached."

As you can imagine, France was no longer a place I was keen to see again. Just when I thought everything had settled down, I was contacted by the powers-that-be and told I would have to go back to Boulogne for an ID parade. 'Ah, no,' I thought. 'Here we go again.' Still, it was a break from duty for a wee while and although I can't say I very much liked going back over there, to cut a long story short, I ended up in an ID parade room. The usual kind of parade – I could see the suspects but the suspects couldn't see me. I pointed out the trigger-happy gentleman, who looked even more like a grim hooligan to me. I can say that now. He's not going to come looking for me now, is he? Or is he?

Soon after the ID parade, I asked what had happened to the charming fellow who had tried to kill me and I was told he just got a ticking off. So, he took a gun to me, filled my rear end full of lead and left me to die in a gutter but all that was just dismissed as a crime of passion. That's France for you. He's probably still over there, with his wife slogging away in the bar for him, and he's probably still keeping a shotgun upstairs in case anyone gets too close. Was I more careful after that escapade? Mais, oui, monsieur. You bet your life I was.

In October 1975 I was coming towards the end of my career in the Royal Navy. I could have signed on again but that was the completion of my five year stint. It was quite an emotional time and there was a going away party arranged for me on HMS Neptune. It was rather larger than I expected. Hundreds of people turned up. I had a lot of friends there; sailors, Wrens, Royal Marines and civilian workers, and people outwith the base. They all came to say their farewells and it was a typical bash, with beer flowing freely. I did my best to control my intake because I wanted to remember the night in years to come. It was a fantastic night and I was given a couple of beautiful presentations – a photograph and a lighter.

The next day, it was off to HMS Cochrane in Rosyth for the formality of signing my discharge papers. In fact, there was another party there that night because some Wrens came over from Faslane to say their farewells all over again. Wasn't that nice of them? I thought so, too. One or two of them hadn't been able make it to the party the previous night so I met them on HMS Cochrane for yet another celebration. It was another emotional night. And then I was off to Edinburgh as a civilian. That felt really strange. No uniform, no orders, no free food, no free accommodation, no mates. And, sadly, no Wrens.

Freedom at last. I could do whatever I wanted in the world. Brilliant. Except it wasn't. Guess what happened? Yes, during the following months, I began to regret the hastiness of my decision to leave the navy. It was a way of life I had been so used to; a hard-working lifestyle which I tried to continue into civvy street but which just didn't work. Back in Dornoch, people gave me funny looks as I tried to continue the forces' lifestyle, and it took a long time to get over the impact of my discharge. It was as though I'd lost my right hand. I was doing some scallop diving with my friend, Alastair Ross, from Bonar Bridge, but for about a year I seriously thought about joining up again and in fact, yes, I did make enquiries, I went down to Faslane and met the boys in the diving team and the commanding officer.

He was sympathetic. However, he said that I had been out for so many months by then that, although I could probably get back in, I would have to re-qualify as a clearance diver. I wouldn't have had any problem getting through but I honestly thought I couldn't go through all those training courses again. No, I wasn't going to put myself through all that rigmarole again to be a clearance diver. Enough, already. There and then, I decided I would just have to make my own way through civvy life. No looking back. Onwards and upwards and all that. What did I do? I made my way back home to Dornoch. Reunited with my parents, I lapsed into the hard-drinking lifestyle for some time until I settled down with the help of my dad, who was a pillar of strength.

He supported me. He understood what I was going through, which was a godsend for me. My mother also helped, but my dad was a man of the world and he understood these things. During my time with the Navy, I had only gone home to Dornoch for, maybe, a long weekend or on leave. I had been very proud to be a member of the Royal Navy and extremely proud of my job, and I was always happy to tell people. They would ask me about my life and it was just great, meeting people when I was back home and talking about explosives and stuff like that. Coming home after my discharge was completely different. Everything just seemed so flat. I hadn't got the same bounce in myself. I really felt deflated. It wasn't long before I realised there would be none of the camaraderie, the laugh-a-minute boozing sessions in the pubs in Faslane or the same crack with the Wrens.

Feeling out on a limb, I didn't want to talk about the Royal Navy anymore. It was just a memory and I felt very sad that I was no longer part of it. All good things come to an end, and I was fighting my own inner feelings. Confused, and trying to continue the laddish life I had lived with the rest of the crew in Faslane, my behaviour wasn't going down too well with my parents and other people in Dornoch. As a civilian, you can't act in the carefree way that service people do when they are not on shift the following morning. A person coming out of the services sticks out like a sore thumb, or that's how they feel, because of the very different life they have led before.

In the Faslane Diving Team, we were a law unto ourselves. Whereas the rest of the service personnel would be out on ceremonial parades, or divisions as we called them, the diving team were out blowing up mines and other exciting tasks. Obviously, there was discipline in the diving team but not the kind of discipline people think of when they look at the services. Because we were an elite group of people we just seemed to get away with far more than ordinary guys in the Royal Navy would. Of course, there had to be discipline in the kind of work we were doing – working with bombs, mines and explosives, but that was instilled into each member of the team. We wouldn't have been in the team if we didn't understand what we were doing or if we just wandered about aimlessly, thinking we were God's gift. Any member of the team who stepped out of line would be severely reprimanded. If the breach was serious enough, they would be dismissed from the diving team. That had happened before so everyone knew their place and, although we worked hard and played hard, we knew our limits. I missed that service life, the certainties it gave us and even those limits on what we could and could not do. To continue living the way I had been living for the previous five years was a lie in itself.

Anyone can go and get plastered and think it's a great way of life. Others can get plastered with you but, in the cold light of day, you've got nothing to go back to. I had lost my comrades, lost my way of life and I felt dead inside. Dad understood these feelings and tried to help me as much as he could. There were others, too, who could see my dilemma and they did step in to try and help me along. It was only when I began diving again that I managed to get back to as near normal a life as I could ever have. Out of the chaos emerged some routine and a sense of responsibility. Things started to get better from then on.

Alastair Ross had started his own diving outfit, the Ross Diving Company. Soon, I had teamed up with him and for the next few years I was back diving around Scotland. Alastair himself was an ex-Merchant Navy seaman, a hardy type. He owned a Land Rover for all the bits and pieces of diving equipment and had regular work from Highland Regional Council, working on their various ferry boat moorings. We dived for the Scottish Hydro Electric Board on various dams throughout Scotland. We also did work for the United Kingdom Atomic Energy Authority in Dounreay.

One job Alastair and I did for the county council was outside the Nigg Hotel, at the old pier. The pier was wooden and they wanted it removed. In cases like that, we usually used a CP9 underwater auger: an air-driven auger suitable for boring holes in piles under water. We would then stuff small sticks of explosives into the holes so that there was a long line of Cordtex with offshoots, going to about half a dozen charges at the base of each pile. We'd then get out of the water, retire to a safe distance and detonate. It was quite spectacular actually; when we detonated the piles they would come shooting out of the water like a Polaris missile. I think we did about 15 of these, if I remember right, and it cleared the way for them to build a new pier.

We began to get regular work at the UKAEA at Dounreay in Caithness. Some of the work was in the complex itself and often involved clearing the grills, or band screens as they were called, in the pumphouses, to stop the weed and whatever else coming in from the sea. Often the screens were damaged during bad weather and a lot of debris would be washed in. We had to remove the damaged screens and measure up for new ones to be fitted. There were also various other tasks to be done, such as filming, photography and repairs. It was mostly all under concrete, working in tidal conditions which meant being swept back and fore while trying to do the job to the best of our ability. It was heavy going but that's what we were there for. Apart from Alastair and myself, we also had to have dive tenders or linesmen, such as Rob Sinclair or the late Cathel Dingwall. A law unto themselves, but great guys who looked after all the dive gear.

We also were required to work on outfall, or effluent, pipes. That's where the waste cooling water from the reactor discharges into the sea. These were found way down, in about 80 feet of water. It was normally quite clear water but the waste coming out of these pipes was very warm and under those conditions you'd find some very odd marine life down there. There were lobsters and conger eels, for example, which grew to rather larger sizes than they would normally. It seemed a bit strange and I soon discovered that the liquid coming out of these pipes obviously wasn't just clean water; there was a lot of radiation contamination too. This was contaminating the whole area around the pipes.

When we worked, we always used one of two fishing boats hired to help us. One was The Prolific and the other, The Primula, skippered by the late Angie Meek and the late Denny Simpson. The skippers knew exactly where these effluent pipes were by navigational points they had on the shore and they would lay down their anchors so the vessel was directly above the work area.

When diving was in progress there were many tasks involved, including building up sandbags beside these pipes to try and protect them from anchors or fishing dredges. There was an exclusion zone around Dounreay and no shellfish were to be taken from the immediate area, for obvious reasons. While we worked offshore at Dounreay we had people with us from the UKAEA who would use geiger counters to monitor the level of contamination on ourselves, as well as our diving suits, and we had what they called film badges attached to us while underwater which would give readings in case we started to glow in the dark. In fact, we regularly had positive readings on these devices when we picked up contamination. An ex-Wren, Heather Rowley, was the monitor, and she used to check us over and make sure we were scrubbed down in the decontamination room in Dounreay. Our diving suits would regularly be taken away and destroyed. Maybe that's why some people still say I have a warm personality.

One day, a pod of killer whales appeared which was thrilling for those on the surface, although the poor diver down below didn't know anything about it. I don't think killer whales go for humans anyway but it was a bonny sight. The poor skipper got so jittery when the whales arrived that he wanted his boat out of there before he got rammed. As it happened, they never bothered with us at all.

Sometimes, when we were looking for effluent pipes they could not be found; although the marks were there, the pipes weren't. They would be buried in shifting sands or bad visibility would prevent us from finding them, and on these occasions we used a machine which we called 'the bomb'. This was a huge brass cylinder with electronics inside. It was a radiation monitor which was dropped down on an umbilical line to the seabed, to detect any radioactive particles, known as hotspots, and relay this information to the surface.

The works officer would point out areas to be checked and down we would go, in the hope of finding our target. That was done many times in various places and we were getting high numbers of hotspot readings over large areas, but no pipes. It actually showed what a huge area was affected. Eventually, we would have to leave because we were either all dived out or the visibility might force us to return the next day when things might have changed. As for those effluent pipes, well, they are still out there. Although the reactor at Dounreay itself is shut down now, a lot of hotspots are still being found to this day and causing concern. I suspect they will be for many years to come.

Another diving job, which came along for me and Alastair after I left the Royal Navy, was at the Nigg oil fabrication yard. A lot of diving work which we did was done around the dock gates, work which included clearing debris away and filming; photography as well as checking valves, bolts and bearing pads. All the big rubber seals around the dock had to be checked and anything that was out of place or slack would have to be fixed. When the whole process was complete, we would film the repairs for the benefit of management, to make sure they were happy. We fitted new ladders, grilles, valves, etc., working closely with engineers who had to monitor what we were doing. I spent several years diving there and was just like part of the regular workforce. We got to know all the crew helping us at the dock and we were on first name terms with them. Things were quite comfortable as we had our own diving unit there, where we could get changed and store our diving gear under lock and key.

Then there was a black day, in February 1978. We had a young diver by the name of Mike Pickering working with us who had recently gone through a diving course and had passed. Mike was one of our divers on-site with Alastair Ross, myself and Rob Sinclair, the linesman tender. Mike was a keen young diver. He wanted to do the dive himself that morning – we had been asked to do a survey before the Transworld oilrig came into the dock and he wanted more experience on the gate. I was the standby diver and was in contact with Mike on the radio. Rob, as tender, was holding the umbilical line. Mike was on surface demand diving equipment and everything seemed under control. While talking to Mike on the radio, I realised he seemed to be getting a bit concerned about his line. I then asked Rob to take up the slack on the umbilical but it shot out of his hands. When I asked what was going on, Rob said he had no idea. I tried to contact Mike several times but got no response and I knew at that point that something serious had gone wrong. As the standby diver, I immediately went in and followed the umbilical down to where I saw it disappear into a narrow pipe of just 18 inches diameter. I went cold.

Grabbing hold of the umbilical, I tried to pull it out. As I did so, my fins slipped off the flange and I was partially sucked into the pipe myself. To this day, I believe that if I hadn't been such a big guy I would have been in there after Mike. However, I managed to release myself and climbed the ladder up onto the dock gate with a growing sense of anger and frustration that I could do nothing to help him. Other divers appeared from the Transworld and it was decided the only way we could get Mike out was to cut open that section of the pipe. This took about 20 hours. Air was supplied all the time and the radio was kept open. We kept calling Mike in case there was any sign of life. While the recovery operation was taking place, everything that could have been done was done to give him a fighting chance. There wasn't supposed to be any suction in those pipes, but through the night, due to some misunderstanding, the valves had been opened without our knowledge. It was a tragic accident, and an experience that deeply affected me. It still haunts me, and I'm sure others also, to this day.

Eager for a change and maybe to see a bit more of the world, I spotted an advert for crew to work on a two-masted schooner brig; an ex-Baltic trader, which was laid up at the Muirtown Lochs at Inverness. They needed a crew for this ship, the Christian Bach, to sail on Pacific Island charters with some very rich people. Thinking I would give it a go, I wrote off to the skipper. He replied asking me to go for an interview. That's how I got a job as a Leading Seaman, down to my naval qualifications and my knowledge of the sea and diving. Crewing was a very strange experience, to say the least. I had never worked on yachts or sailing ships before.

Dealing with rigging and ropes was something new to me. This particular sailing ship had been bought by Chris Henderson, an Australian gentleman. I don't know how much he paid for it but his ambition was to run Pacific charters. He planned to convert the

Christian Bach into a luxury sailing ship with thickly carpeted cabins and the best of furniture, bedding and so on.

Our job as the crew, apart from learning the finer points of seamanship, was to help the joiners and carpenters fit new yardarms, under the watchful eye of the foreman, Duncan Forbes. We had to climb up to the mast, and if you didn't have a head for heights, it was a pretty frightening experience. I did okay at it. Sea cadets were brought on board but no lifelines or safety harnesses of any kind were provided. I thought that pretty strange health and safety practice, even then. One of the more switched-on cadets, a young guy called Steve Turnbull, was doing a lot of work up top. Being very concerned the guy could fall and seriously hurt himself, I brought my fears to the attention of the skipper.

His reply was that when we were out in the Pacific we would all have to learn the hard way. There would, he said, be no time for all the safety harness stuff. He was planning to have some of these guys go hand over hand, along some steel wire rope between the two masts at the top, without any safety harnesses. I was shocked. It didn't happen because I stepped in. I thought it was a really crazy idea. The skipper backed down but by this time I had the feeling that he was sailing off to cloud cuckoo land. Just to confirm my suspicions, Henderson arrived one day in a Royal Navy uniform with a big cutlass hanging by his side. That, and he wanted the whole crew to start wearing naval uniforms. Having not long left the navy myself, I found it all a bit strange. By this time, I was not just suspicious but having second thoughts about being within a mile of this character, who was supposed to be in charge of us. We weren't even being properly paid for being on the ship – just £10 to £15 a week, enough to get you a couple of pints at the weekend, although we were being fed.

The only thing that stopped me leaving was seeing myself on Pacific charters with paying guests, as the Christian Bach sailed in endless sunshine on beautiful, blue seas. So I decided to stick with it. One night the police came along and said that a storage unit holding some of our liferafts had been broken into and some medicines were missing, including morphine. We were all interviewed about it. I had no idea what was going on. The skipper, Chris Henderson, was asked some serious questions but said later that he had a lot of friends in the police in Inverness, and in other organisations, and that everything would be sorted. It was. We heard no more about it. He was a strange guy who used to sleep with some sort of Magnum pistol under his pillow. Another night, some people came near the ship and he started firing shots at the side of the pier. The police were involved again but, again, nothing happened.

Things began to take shape on board. Cabins were ready, the rattlings and the riggings were looking good, and the sails were taken on, hoisted and purled. It was a steep learning curve. I enjoyed it, even though I had a lot of reservations about the barmy skipper and one or two of the crew, who thought the sun shone out of his you-know-what. They obviously had little knowledge of seamanship themselves. However, I was sticking with it. It then occurred to me that we should have a medic on board. What would happen if someone became seriously ill on board, or if someone was to break a leg or develop appendicitis? Chris Henderson said, "I will be the medic."

'Hmm,' I thought to myself. 'Was he qualified? What if someone aboard needed an operation?' This was all getting a bit too much for me. I didn't ask to see any of his medical equipment. He had thought it through, he said, and had acquired pain-killing gas. It was the type of gas used in hospitals for people who had suffered burns, or for pain relief during childbirth. Not particularly useful for a hand hanging off or a broken leg, however. Incredibly, Chris then decided to demonstrate his expertise with gas on our young cadet, Steven Turnbull. Chief engineer John Grant, also an ex-Navy guy, had also expressed his reservations about what could happen. Soon after, John and I were below decks while still alongside at Muirtown Docks when we heard this howling and screaming. We went along to investigate and found the skipper cauterising a wart on Steve's hand. He said he was 'just experimenting' with the pain-killing gas and thought he'd cauterise the poor fellow's hand with a red-hot poker.

"Look, I gave him the gas and he's doing fine now."

Alas, the poor lad was far from fine. He was in absolute agony and needed proper medical attention. We all knew by now that the skipper was raving bonkers but we wanted our trip to the sun.

A television crew came along one day, from the ITV children's programme, Magpie. Our skipper, of course, was in his glory, strutting about in his uniform and showing off his cutlass. The crew had to be there in uniform – jumpers and shirts and each of us wearing a black beret. He said he wanted the TV crew piped on board the ship.

"Hey, hold on," I said. "That is not the sort of thing you do. Piping on board should only to be done for senior Royal Navy Officers and dignitaries."

I knew that. However, Henderson asked me to do the honours. I refused point blank. No way. No bloody way. The simple reason was that I would be seen on television. No self-respecting ex-Royal Navy rating would pipe a TV crew on board any vessel. It was not the done thing and my training told me it was wrong. When I watched the programme afterwards, I cringed. I was very glad I had not taken part in that farce.

There were many other strange decisions made, too. Like the time Chris Henderson decided he wanted to take the ship onto Loch Ness for a sea trial. Although not on board myself at that point, I had been told there were writs pinned to the mast. When a writ is delivered in that manner it means the ship can't go anywhere. The owner owes a lot of money to someone and the vessel is being held. The rumour was that he owed about a quarter of a million pounds.

Regardless of the writs, I steered the ship up to Loch Ness. The Christian Bach had an engine as well as sails and she was beautiful on passage. Her engine was one of her best features. It was a single cylinder job and to start it, pressurised air was used to turn a massive flywheel beside the engine. We used the engine to get us through the Caledonian Canal and eventually into Loch Ness. This was all taking place during the festive season and I had told the skipper I wanted to go home for New Year. He wasn't going to let me off the ship but I demanded the ship be taken to Foyers Pier and reluctantly, he let me go. That was my break and, the way events were developing, I was glad to get off that boat.

It was dark when I disembarked and off I went, trying to hitch a lift to Inverness to catch the last train up to Ardgay. I'll never forget that stretch of road – I knew there was a big house down on the left hand side which had been owned, many years before, by a strange man who went by the name of Aleister Crowley. Rumour had it that he was into the occult and all that stuff, and the house was called Boleskine House. It had subsequently been bought by Led Zeppelin guitarist, Jimmy Page, who was also into all kinds of unusual stuff. As I passed the house I got a weird feeling. It was one of those dark nights; the wind was blowing, and seeing that old house at the side of the road, I could have sworn there was a light flickering inside. Was someone beckoning me in? Whether it was a figment of my imagination or not, I don't really know. I didn't stop long enough to find out. I scooted along that road until I got well past Boleskine. Looking back, I suppose my imagination was working overtime because I knew the house had belonged to Crowley and I had heard so much about him and the occult. Eventually, I managed to get a lift and, joy of joys, I was soon home for the festivities.

Once Christmas and New Year were over, I made my way back to the Muirtown Basin and the Christian Bach. The first people I met coming on board were the engineer, John Grant, and his good wife, Trish. Poor old Trish was in tears. She wasn't happy about her husband returning to the ship and she made her views known to me. She was a lovely lady and I understood what she was saying and said I would speak to her husband in due course about what was going on. By then the Christian Bach had done her trials in Loch Ness and we continued preparing her for the South Pacific. I had brought my diving gear when I returned and the skipper wanted the bottom of the ship checked out. It was copper-plated, as was normal for a vessel of that type, to stop the sea worms eating through her bottom. I gave her a thorough check over and no serious problems were found.

We continued with the rigging and kitting out of the ship, but I think one of the skipper's main concerns was the crew's conduct on board and how we were turned out. It was more important to him how we looked to the public than what was actually far more important – the proper running of the ship itself. I continued for about another four weeks and then things came to a head between me and the skipper. It was very obvious to me he was not a fit or capable person to make the necessary rational decisions to ensure the safety of the ship and everyone on board. I was not happy to stay on board any longer. I told Mr Henderson I wasn't happy to continue and that I had signed no contract to come onto the ship, so I was signing no contract to leave. I walked the plank and left him to his own devices, and I was followed off by the Chief Engineer.

A strong sense of relief swept through me when I left because I knew that the way things were going, the Christian Bach would never actually make it as a charter ship in the Pacific under that man. There was something wrong about the whole setup; it just wasn't good at all. After this, I heard various rumours about the Christian Bach – the last one being was that it was seen being escorted up the Thames into London by the police. I don't know if that was true and I don't really care, apart from the passing interest of having worked on it.

I have been in contact with somebody who took photographs on board the ship in Edinburgh before it was bought by Chris Henderson. However, a little online research has shown me that the interesting life of the ship continued. Henderson, it seems, did not make it to the Pacific as he sold to new owners a year or two after I quit. No surprise there. Renamed the Lillebjoern, she went on a voyage from Panama to the Galapagos Islands with some youngsters who are described in the article I found as 'having schooling problems'. A report said that at one stage she was set on fire by the unruly young crew and for a fortnight they drifted about the Pacific 'with engine failure and a group of violent pupils unwilling to accept any authority from neither crew nor other staff'. Among other alarming incidents, the pupils attempted felling the main mast with the fire axe, and apparently the damage they did to the wooden fore deck is still evident. In 1990 she was renamed Spirit of Winestead for another school, and there is little trace of her after that. I still wonder what happened to her.

CHAPTER 4

In January 1979, I was down in Fife again, with the Ross Diving Company. We were staying in Kinghorn and doing diving work for the water board. That particular month there was serious frost. We had a lot of problems getting through the ice into the dams and reservoirs and it was difficult to complete a lot of the work needed. Our air hoses were freezing up and we were diving under the ice. Eventually, we had to pack in the diving altogether because the frost was causing problems with the diving gear and affecting safety. We packed up our stuff to head back north again.

We got underway and soon Alastair stopped by a telephone box to tell his wife Irene we were heading home. That was when she told him that my father had passed away. I always remember being at the side of the Land Rover that day, throwing snowballs at him, but when he came out of the box he had a look about him and I thought, 'Oops, he's not amused.' He walked over slowly and said he was sorry to tell me that Dad had died. That was one of the biggest shocks I have ever had in my whole life. My father had some health problems, stemming from the time he had been involved in an accident in my older brother's car. Dad had not been wearing a seatbelt and went through the windscreen which had caused leg, chest and eye injuries. Dad, being Dad, was never one to moan. He just got on with it. Just before his death, he was supposed to have seen somebody about the chest pains he was having. But it never happened.

It was a long journey back up north. The boys tried to get me on a train but they were disrupted due to the weather. So we ploughed through and eventually reached Dornoch where I had to meet the rest of my family and friends and organise the funeral. It really was a very hard time. I'd say my father was the mainstay of my life, he was such a great gentleman and such a great loss, and I felt completely empty for a long time after that.

At the time I had friends, the Smith family, who owned the Trentham Hotel just outside Dornoch. Bob Smith and I decided to raise money for a local charity, an old folk's hospital outside Dornoch by the name of Cambusavie Old Folks Unit. I came up with a plan to swim the Dornoch Firth. Bob wasn't sure about it at first but soon said, "Let's do it."

Another fellow who agreed to take part was Ian Grant (we called him Proncie), from Pitgrudy Farm, just outside Dornoch, who was a very fit, able and eager fellow and he was also the Big Drummer in the Dornoch Pipe Band. The Dornoch Firth is about 12 miles long and the swim could only be done by entering the water at high tide and going out with the ebb. However, we couldn't just float out; we had to swim flat out with fins because otherwise we would not be finished the swim before the tide turned. We had about five and a half hours before the tide would be fully out and the swim had to happen in that time span. I wanted to start the swim by jumping off Bonar Bridge. When I mentioned that to the boys I just got some very strange looks because it's a long way down from the bridge to the surface. After some humming and hawing, they reluctantly agreed to make the leap if I promised to check under the water for any hidden dangers. Of course, I had intended to do that anyway.

Once all the arrangements were made, the media was informed and on the day, crowds gathered on the bridge. The sponsorship forms were sorted out and filled in. We appeared on the bridge in black wetsuits although I think Bob, who sadly is no longer with us, had a yellow one on and must have looked a bit peculiar. No matter, he had the guts to do the swim. I was up first and the crowd wanted to see me jump off the bridge. Geronimo! I hit that water like a bullet then waited for the others to follow me in. The firth weaves and winds its way round to Dornoch and Tain and is certainly not a straight stretch of water. Prior to the swim I had checked the maps and initially, the boys followed me round the channels and everything was going fine. The safety boats were working with us and everything was tickety-boo. Then the lads began falling behind and I wondered whether to wait for them or should I just go for it. I knew if I didn't, I probably wouldn't complete the swim. I told the crew on the safety boat that I was going on ahead. Swimming down the Dornoch Firth, there were a lot of strong tides and a lot of inquisitive seals as well, popping up beside me to pass the time of day.

It was very misty towards the middle of the firth and another safety boat, a large inflatable, skippered by Jimmy Macdonald and a lassie called Kate Appleton, were there to look after me. I asked what had happened to the other safety vessel as I hadn't seen it for some time. They said the boys on that boat had gone to get a carry-out about half way down the firth. But the tide was going out and they were beached and stuck there. Jimmy and Kate were with me all the way down the firth to the Gisen Briggs. Once I reached the quicksands there, I had done my bit and completed the task and they got me on board. I had taken about six hours and that was constant swimming, apart from taking a wee drink of water here and there. Jimmy and Kate took me to the beach at Dornoch. It was very cold; a fog had come in and there were just a few people on the beach to meet us. No one had actually known where I was going to land. The others made it about half way down to Meikle Ferry and there was a crowd to meet them – all asking where the heck I was. They had no idea and just said I was away ahead. We all met up later in the Trentham Hotel and had a fantastic night. In the end we raised a lot of money for the old folks unit. It was the first time the Dornoch Firth had ever been swum and I don't think it has ever been attempted again since. Now that I have drawn attention to this, perhaps it will be soon. But I was the first to conquer the firth and, yes, I am rather happy I did it.

It was after my dip in the firth that I got the offer of my first offshore diving job with Subsea International, and had to go to Aberdeen for a medical before I could take the job. That was an eventful job because, while I am not what you would call an activist in the workplace, I did get the sack during a period of industrial unrest. It happened on the

Ninian Northern platform, a good bit north, off Shetland. It was good diving work where we used hot water suits which had a hot water hose in the umbilical line. The heated water was pumped through veins in the diving suit so we were working in a lovely, cosy, warm environment and wearing commercial Kirby Morgan band masks or helmets, depending on what we were doing. The work involved surface decompression. In other words, we would go down, do the work with power tools, air tools: grinding, welding, photography, burning or filming. When we came back up to the surface we had three minutes to get our suit off and into the chamber where we were blown back down to a certain depth, breathing pure oxygen part of the time as the air pressure was gradually reduced in the decompression chamber.

There was one day on this job when I was asked to get the guys ready for diving by the supervisors, one of whom was Alastair Ross. Alastair had previously been my boss when I worked for his company, Ross Diving. Now he was one of the regular crew on the Ninian Northern but he was also a saturation diver, a hardy type. The guys I was working with knew that Alastair was a friend and one of them turned round and said to me, "No, we are not doing it. We're not diving."

I asked why not and he said they were on strike. They hadn't told me because they reckoned I would pass it on to others further up the chain. Everything came to an abrupt halt and I had to go and report to the dive superintendent that we were on strike. The British Professional Divers Association, it has to be said, had wound their way into the minds of a lot of the divers. It was all about gripes they had with foreign divers taking over a lot of the work that our own guys should have been getting. That certainly was happening. British divers couldn't go to some other countries, like Australia and New Zealand, and do the same thing or they would have been chucked out. They probably wouldn't have been allowed in, in the first place. It happened because our government had caved in and was also the fault of the industry itself, so I couldn't blame these guys. However, I don't know who instigated the strike. I only know there was no more diving. I am afraid that, try as we might, we couldn't change these guys' minds. No matter what I said, it made no difference whatsoever.

As time went on, we were threatened with disciplinary action by management and the next thing we knew, the strike action had spread and there was industrial action in Aberdeen. It never came to much but eventually we had to leave the oil platform and I was back home. It was very disappointing, what happened. It was a job I enjoyed but I received letters confirming that I, and everyone involved in the dispute, had been sacked. That made me furious because it was so unfair. I had had nothing to do with the actual dispute. What really riled me was that the shore-based divers kept their jobs, yet they were the ones who had instigated the entire strike. Us boys who were working offshore, were only doing what we were told but we lost our jobs. That was not only annoying – I found it quite sickening as well. Subsea International was a company I really enjoyed working for because they were a very professional outfit and I'm saddened that my involvement with the company ended in the way it did.

After I finished with Subsea in 1983, I was lucky enough to get a job with Oceaneering, another strong diving outfit in Aberdeen, and I started off working with them at Invergordon. We worked on the maintenance of oilrigs; a lot of them would come in and anchor off Invergordon. It was a case of surveying each one and carrying out repairs – whatever was required. We worked on the likes of the Hutton TLP (tension leg platform) out in the Moray Firth. That was quite a deep job, diving some 120 feet down and then swimming up about 20 feet inside the legs to get to the job. Interesting work. I did this for some time until I said I would like to go offshore. Soon, I was off to the North Sea. They sent me to dive support ships mostly, including the Rigmaster, the Willchief and the Stena Constructor. We went to the Vallhall field, off Norway, doing some habitat work on the legs of some of the structures there. Then we were in Nam field, off the Dutch coast for a while, doing work on a gas pipeline. That continued right up until 1986 when I was sent up to Sinclair Bay in Wick.

There is a construction yard there where pipelines are built, to be towed into the North Sea, and our job was to set out the ballast on the pipeline as it was sailed out. There were huge, steel shackles suspended from different parts of the pipeline and to get the ballast right, some of the shackles had to be cut off and some had to be added on. It was real balancing act to ensure the pipeline was towed out to sea at a certain depth. Initially, I dealt with the shallow water work, only diving to about 30 to 50 feet. As the pipeline was towed further out, it would be dropped down to about 60 feet.

On one job, I was told they needed me to go out to the tow head which was situated at the deeper end of the pipeline, right out where there were extremely strong tides. The head of the pipeline was under about 140 feet of water and I asked why they needed me out there. They said there were only two divers they would trust going down to do the job on air and the other diver had run out of time, trying to remove the pin from a shackle which was holding the pipeline in place. I asked about the size and all they said was that the shackle pin was big. Big? Could they give me some indication? They said the pin itself probably weighed about a few hundred pounds – so it was obvious the shackle weighed about a ton. That time, I was diving from a Smit-Lloyd ship, one of the larger dive support vessels out in the North Sea. Before we did anything we had to have a proper briefing. It's all very well saying, "OK, I'll do this," but if you are not 100% sure about what is going on then that's when problems start.

The other diver was Dave Conners, a local man from Wick. He had managed to unscrew the shackle and fit a wire through the eye of the pin but the eye had snapped. So the shackle was still in place. The pipeline was big: miles long. With tides being the way they were, I would have to stay in the dive basket until such time as I saw the pipeline and there was slack water, or I would just be swept off the job. The surface team fitted the wire strop with a small shackle to the bottom end of it. Down I went. The job could only be done in slack tide and there were only a few minutes of it in Sinclair Bay. I got down to maybe 30 or 40 feet when the basket was almost turned horizontal. The tides were whipping it away and I couldn't do anything about it. I reported that the basket, with me in it, should be taken back up on board, pronto. We were on an umbilical so the air was coming from a surface supply, along with the communications. They winched me back up to the ship to rethink the tide systems strategy. The next slack water was going to be around midnight and they were going to have to time it absolutely perfectly, just to get me down before the tide had actually stopped running. I'd be in about 140 feet of water as the tide slackened off, which would give me a few minutes to do the job when I got there. I had lights on my helmet and a hand torch also. Come midnight, they lowered me in the dive basket and everything seemed calm. I continued down and it was quite a fast descent because I wanted to get the job done as quickly as possible.

Down to 140 feet where, luckily, I could see the end of the pipeline because it was painted yellow. That helped. It was around 10 feet below me, swinging about quite a bit. I swam down to the shackle, got a hold of the strop and took a look at the situation. I could see where the pin had been unscrewed but the eye had snapped. Obviously, Dave Connors had done a great job. I took a turn around the pin with the wire, shackled it back on to itself and instructed topside to take the strain. But there was some problem with communication and by the time that happened, the tide was starting to run again. The seconds were ticking by. Every second counts in a situation like that and if the tide became too strong I would have to abort the whole operation. As luck would have it, communications came back and I told the guys again to take the strain on the wire – but gently.

I was on the top of the pipeline, hanging on to the flange and watching the strain on the pin, at about as safe a distance as I could be from it. The pin parted company with the shackle and I thought, 'Job done.' I hadn't reckoned on what happened next. The pin had come out, but the shackle did not part from the towing hawser. Everything seemed to freeze in place and there was nothing I could do. The tide was starting to run and the pin was beginning to swing because of the swell on the surface. I wasn't particularly happy about this lump of steel flying up and down beside me. One blow from it and I would have been as dead as a dodo in a frogman's suit. So I radioed the guys to get it out of the way. Looking back now, I am very glad that I did.

They lifted the basket back up to the surface and removed the pin while I was still 140 feet down. I was watching that shackle, still attached to the pipeline, and it was so huge and so heavy that there was nothing I could have done to move it. With the tide starting to flow, the shackle began to move back and fore and I could see that it was eventually going to come away. Time to get out of there. I requested the dive basket to be sent back down but I really wasn't prepared for what happened next. The massive shackle came away from the pipeline with a loud crack. The whole pipeline shuddered then lurched up towards the surface. Unfortunately, yours truly was still pinned on top of the pipe with the umbilical wrapped round me, right up until it stabilised at about a depth of 80 feet.

We missed the basket by inches. I was rather lucky that they did not connect. Shouting at me via the radio, dive control asked what the hell was I doing at 80 feet? Never mind that, guys; just haul the basket up to my depth and take in the slack umbilical. I made it clear in unparliamentary language that I was not going to answer daft questions until they got me out of there and into the decompression chamber. They understood I wasn't messing; the basket arrived and I clambered in and instructed them to haul away. Due to the severe tide then running, there were problems with the flailing umbilical which was wrapping itself around the basket. I was winched on board as fast as possible, put into the chamber, then pressurised down to depth. Control kept asking why the hell I had been at that depth. I was not in the mood. I told them to shut up as I was on O2 and trying to get myself relaxed while decompressing. After a while I told them what had happened and there was silence. Someone swore a bit and then said well done. Then someone else asked why I hadn't bothered to recover the shackle. My answer is unprintable.

So what had caused me to be catapulted up to 80 feet? The pipe was a large, metal offshore oil pipe which was full of air, so once the shackle attached to the towing hawser came away from the end of the pipe, it decided to do its own thing and make its way up. Nobody had warned me anything like that could happen. They didn't know themselves. Had anyone considered that possibility, we would have had to rethink the whole operation because it was so dangerous. That dive would not have been considered until a risk assessment had been carried out. Anyway, muggins here went down and proved the hard way what can go wrong.

On another occasion, I remember Northern Constabulary calling on the services of Ross Diving Company to search for someone's luggage at the bottom of the River Brora, under the railway bridge. There had been a spate of thefts in the Wick area and around Caithness. The police had narrowed the culprit down to one particular guy who was seen going onto a train at Wick which was then stopped by the police at Brora. As the cops stopped it, the suspect was seen throwing a suitcase out the window and into the river.

When Alastair went down to search for the case, he came across a German field gun. We were a bit staggered by this at first. It transpired that the gun had been presented to the people of Brora after being captured from a German detachment during the war. Another one had been given as a memento to Dornoch and promptly relegated to the bottom of the witches pool. And the good folk of Brora hadn't really fancied having to look at a piece of German armoury every day either so they had tossed it over the side of the bridge and into the River Brora. Lying beside the gun was the case that the cops were so keen to examine. It was recovered, taken to the surface and to the car park, where a squad of Northern Constabulary's finest were waiting to see if it was full of goodies that had been purloined all around Caithness. Perhaps they should have realised from the ease with which the diver brought it to the surface that the case wasn't that heavy. TV cameras were rolling and everyone was waiting with bated breath. Lo and behold, they opened the suitcase and what did they find? A load of women's underwear: bras and pants which had been nicked off a washing line. It wasn't quite what the forces of law and order were looking for and a bit of an embarrassment for them with so many observers looking expectantly on.

Alastair Ross and I then went to Stockholm to work on a project based on a concept devised by one of our divers, Martin Dane, ex-RN. Coincidentally, his son Richard (or Tricky), also ex-RN, is now a SAR Commander in Stornoway. Small world. Martin was a very bright man and always had lots of great practical ideas. He was a bit of an inventor, actually. He came up with an idea about how to transport a diver through hot oil in caverns. He was all set to patent it, too. All the oil in Sweden was held in underground caverns, you see. Under the oil there were pumps which were set in fresh water. To pump oil out of them you had to pump fresh water in, and those pumps needed maintenance from time to time. The caverns had to be emptied of oil, which was a big job, and I suppose all the pumps would have to be degreased before they could even be worked on. Martin's solution was a device which would transport the diver through the hot oil and into the fresh water below. It was a large perspex box, in the shape of a coffin actually, large enough for one diver to lie in. Water hoses cooled the coffin all the time. The container would be lowered into the cavern, through the hot oil. The diver would have high-powered torches with him and a cling-film-type seal on his mask. If any oil got onto the mask he would be able to peel the seal off when he reached the fresh water. The depth of the oil could be anything up to 80 feet so it was quite a daunting feat. It was all tested out in miniature and Martin had connections in Stockholm who were prepared to undertake a full-size experiment. An agent arranged for us to go over to try out the contraption.

Martin, Alastair and I were taken down to a yard where we were shown the perspex box and the lifting sling all set up. We were eager to get to one of these hot oil caverns just for the experience. However, it never happened because the contacts in Sweden didn't have the correct equipment. Cranes and winches of a very high standard were needed, as well as suits to keep us cool. There was supposed to have been a standby diver fully equipped to go in, if necessary, too. None of this had been arranged so the whole thing came to an abrupt end. During our time in Stockholm however, we enjoyed taking in the sights of that fair city. We had a great time.

I remember while travelling across to Stockholm on the ferry that there were a lot of football fans going over as well. I like football to a certain extent, but I'm no dedicated fan. For instance, I don't know many top footballers. Anyway, we were taken to this club called The Tudor Arms, in Stockholm. Great place. We were having a fantastic afternoon there. I do remember, though, that the beer was very expensive. But we enjoyed the atmosphere and gassing about what might have been with the job we had come to do.

A bunch of English lads came into the bar and Alastair Ross got chatting to them, I thought they were probably football supporters. One of them came across and started chatting to me. His name was Alan and he asked if I was across for the football match.

"What football match?"

He said, "Oh, you're not a fan?"

I told him I knew little about the beautiful game and explained that we were there for a diving job. He seemed very interested and was asking all about the whys and wherefores of diving, about treasure and wrecks. In the middle of our conversation, some guy came up behind me and I felt a sharp blow to the back of the head. Stunned, I went down. The guy then started beating the whatyoumaycallit out of me. As I came to, I began to retaliate and eventually had him on the ground. I walloped him. Sorry, but I did. And then I thumped him again, harder. I had no idea what was going on but the rest of the guys ploughed in too. One of them got hold of this character and another grabbed me, and after they had worked out what had happened, my aggressive new acquaintance was chucked out in the street. For the life of me I couldn't understand why he had hit me. Alastair had actually seen the action, and I told him I had just been speaking to an English guy, big Alan, who I thought was a supporter, when this idiot had come up behind me and attacked me.

Alastair said, "Chris, the guy you were talking to plays for England!"

England were playing Sweden in some World Cup thing. Alastair said, "They're all members of the England football team. They're not supporters. This is the team, mate."

Oh, was it? Alastair apologised to the rest of those guys for me, saying, "I'm sorry but Chris doesn't know anything about football." Then he looked at me and said, "Big Alan, as you call him, is Alan Ball, the footballer."

Now, I had heard of Alan Ball but I didn't know who he was or what he looked like. And he hadn't gone out of his way to say, "I am Alan Ball, I am a famous footballer." He wasn't pushy in any way. We had talked about various things but he obviously didn't want it to be known that he was a famous footballer or that they were the England team. A very modest guy. When everyone found out what had happened, we all had a good laugh. I suppose I was a bit of laughing stock because of my ignorance – not that it was held against me. I was taken under the team's wing for the rest of the day. I didn't have to buy a drink for the rest of afternoon and I went home rejoicing. The guy who had attacked me had done so because he thought I was taking the mickey out of Alan Ball. As if. He'd heard me saying I wasn't a football fan, that I knew nothing about football and wasn't across there to watch any football team. In his befuddled state, he thought I was some kind of enemy. He didn't believe I knew nothing about football. Most people get into trouble because they know and say too much about football, but I got a smack simply for not knowing anything at all about it.

That trip to Sweden was in the early 1980s and it was in 1984 that I got married. I was still diving offshore during that period and I had met a girl, Shona Gunn, from Halkirk in Caithness. Her parents, Hamish and Heather, were both teachers up in that neck of the woods and she had two sisters, Hazel and Eileen. They were a lovely family. We got married and decided to move from Dornoch to Stornoway to live. Shona was in the police and was transferred to Stornoway. It made no difference to me where I lived, I would just take whatever work I could pick up, and I could easily go offshore from Stornoway rather than Dornoch.

Eventually, the diving work began to dry up and I was really looking for something else while finding other ways to pass my time. I like birds – of all kinds. However, I am not what you would call a twitcher. Despite that, in August 1985 I joined John Murdo Macleod, or Iosdaidh (pronounced Ee-yus-dee), as he was known, and four ornithologists, as a crew member on a charter to the islands of North Rona, Sulasgeir, Flannans and St Kilda. It was a small, steel-hulled boat called The Shona, with quite a powerful engine. We left in fine weather from the west side of Lewis and headed for North Rona. The weather was normally quite calm in August but I don't think I would have chanced going at any other time of the year in such a small vessel. We got to North Rona where the guys were doing bird counts. Exactly how they did that without counting the same gugas and puffins over and over again, I'm not quite sure. There had been a survey some years previously and they were comparing the figures. It didn't really mean a lot to me but we went round Rona a few times as they scribbled furiously. From Rona we went up to Sulasgeir which, of course, is the place for gugas: the delicacy that is the young gannet. They found there had been no change in the guga population and seemed happy with that.

It took a couple of days to cover the area, climbing onto the rocks, taking photographs and so on. As well as doing the bird count, they had to survey the island itself and see what kind of environment the seabirds were living in. From Sulasgeir, we went off to the Flannan Isles and I really enjoyed the trip across there. When we had completed those islands, I went ashore on the main island and spent a number of hours letting my mind wander about the mysterious story of the missing lighthouse keepers. It was a strange feeling as I thought about how the lighthouse keepers had gone missing in December 1900 and the various theories there were about what happened to them. It was probably a tidal wave that swept them away but people still wonder and let their imaginations run riot. We had a great trip. I had time to dive around the Flannans, which was a real bonus. From there it was on to St Kilda, quite a long way round. The weather was flat calm. Beautiful. Whales and sharks came up to say hello and we saw lots of wildlife on passage between the islands. We reached St Kilda and steamed into Village Bay, initially. After a hearty meal, we discussed with the ornithologists exactly what we were going to do, how long it was going to take and what kind of timeline they had for various species, and so on. Most of each day was spent doing a section at a time, from the boat, and at the end of each day we would head back into Village Bay and in the late afternoon we would all go ashore. I really enjoyed spending time on St Kilda. It's such a magical place.

I would tramp up to the tops of the hills with the ornithologists and it was breathtaking, looking down on to the bay where people had once lived but which is now uninhabited, apart from a few Army and National Trust people. In those days, there was a pub there called The Puff Inn. The army ran that pub like a NAAFI – not too expensive to have a pint or two. I am not too sure what the opening hours were. I don't seem to remember too much about that for some reason. Sadly, The Puff Inn has closed now, but don't let that put you off if you get a chance to visit one of the few unspoilt corners of Europe. We stayed on St Kilda for about a week and a half until such time as all this birdie stuff was over and done with. At the end of each day we would have a meal on the base, if I remember rightly, and then head up to the pub again. Apart from the army and ourselves, there were a lot of civilian guys doing construction work at the base at the time, so they filled the bar and had tales to tell of what they did in the South of England. It was brilliant and we had a fantastic time there, but we eventually had to leave that beautiful place and return to Stornoway.

I happened to be in the pub one night, this time the upstairs lounge of the Clachan Bar in Stornoway, with some of the town worthies, including Kenny Fags and Horace Capaldi. No longer with us, either of them, but if you knew much about the Isle of Lewis you would know that fine pair. I met a guy with them, called Iain Marvin. Iain asked if I had seen an advert in the Stornoway Gazette about Bristow Helicopters looking for aircrew, like engineers and winchmen. I thought he was joking – working in a helicopter was the kind of job I could only dream of.

"You're pulling my leg, aren't you?"

"No," he said and disappeared. He came back with the paper and there was the advert. Ideas began swirling in my head. I wrote straight away to Bristow Helicopters in Aberdeen. In fact, I phoned them as well – just to make myself known to as many people as I could. I didn't hear back. So I phoned a few more times, and eventually I was put in touch with a chief engineer and I told him that I was very interested in a job as a winchman.

He was coming across to Stornoway to do some interviews and asked if I would be available for a chat. Any time, any place, I assured him. And then . . . well, nothing. After a week and a half, I started writing and phoning again. I made a pest of myself because I was sure that someone would eventually say, "For God's sake, get that man off our back, someone see him or do something with him because we are fed up getting these phone calls all the time."

After what seemed an age, the chief engineer phoned back. The interview would be at the Seaforth Hotel and I turned up there all splogged up, with some of the Bristow staff. There were engineers, aircrew and so on: most of them ex-Royal Navy guys. The panel asked me a lot of questions about what they had seen in my CV, including that I had been a joiner once upon a time. They then said that they would take me on as a joiner for a year and, if I kept the hangar floor clean, kept the helicopter clean and kept my nose clean then, perhaps, just maybe, they would consider me for training as a winchman. What? I asked why they wanted me as a carpenter/joiner. They said someone had to build the offices in the hangar and do the conversion work. "And you are the very man for it, Mr Murray."

I had taken all my logbooks and diving certificates but they weren't required − not for cleaning the bloody hangar floor, they weren't. So it was that me and Colin Mackenzie from Ranish were taken on as labourers. We started work on the same day. This was before the helicopter had arrived on station, remember, so the job was to get the base at Stornoway Airport set up and ready. And a jolly fine job we did too, building those offices, having partitions installed as well as making workbenches for the engineers. We ordered it, cut it, built it, painted it and finished it. Then the first helicopter arrived. Call sign Victor Alpha, as it was known. There was a lot of excitement that day. There were no markings on that helicopter, not even 'Coastguard'. It was a Sikorsky S61N, the civilian version of the famous Sea Kings which the RAF and RN had used in the skies over the Hebrides for many a year.

The job then became all about getting all the equipment necessary organised, from the search and rescue kit: the hoists and medical gear, to everything else needed on board. Soon the rescue missions got underway and I continued in the role of carpenter / joiner / labourer / handyman / wiper up-er for the next year; working on the ground, in the offices, helping with all the helicopter kit and with the maintenance tasks. It wasn't what you would call skilled, or even technical. Often, I was just manhandling stuff but what kept me going was a winchman-op called Steve Branley, an ex-Fleet Air Arm veteran, who was very happy to spend time with me and explain the ins and outs of SAR. That was just brilliant and I was just itching to get started.

They were a great bunch of lads down there. Some were ex-Royal Navy or ex-RAF, a right mixture. Then, it happened. After that first year, I was told I would finally be getting my winchman training. Way-hey! Another search and rescue base was being set up at Lee-on-Solent and one of the winchmen, Mick Rowsell, was being transferred to help with the setting up of the base there. Before he headed off south, my training began. One day I was just told to put on a winchman's suit. From then on it was a slow conversion, from what I had been doing on the ground to getting airborne and used to the rescue gear, getting to know to the aircrews, the radio and, eventually, dangling on the end of the wire.

It was a slow start but I was really happy with the way things were going. The aircrew noticed I was very eager to learn, but everything had to be done properly to make sure this keen-as-mustard, albeit inexperienced, airman got it right. Soon I was off to the Robert Gordon's Institute of Technology (RGIT) College in Aberdeen for my medical training. You just can't jump into a job like that but it was appreciated that I was an ex-Royal Navy diver which really helped. It wasn't a big shock to me to be in that type of safety-conscious environment.

My chief trainer at that time was Jeff Todd, a winchman and winch operator, who was a very keen golfer. Another trainer was Mike Langford, and there was Gordon Davis too. Training was heavy going but very enjoyable and after completing all the training I then had tests to take, which I passed, and eventually came the day where I was to go out on search and rescue missions with the boys. I wasn't a fully-fledged winchman, of course, as I was still a bit green. I still had to train as a third member, going down with the crewman winchman, but I was learning the trade. Alighting on boats was good fun. I had to deal with casualties, putting into practice all I had learned in Aberdeen, and working out how to do it all by myself. Then there were the techniques for pumping out boats that were sinking, and carrying out mountain rescue. Though I say it myself, I took to it like a duck to water. Then came the big day. I was a proper winchman and had to go it alone. There was nobody else to back me up or check that I was doing everything correctly. That was the start of my career in search and rescue.

Before I talk about the actual rescues I took part in, how about a wee bit of history? The reason for having a rescue helicopter based in Stornoway actually goes back to a tragic incident in 1985. There was a tragedy involving a Banff-registered fishing boat, called the Bon Ami, on December 19. All six crew were lost. She struck a rock known as Minister's Point, a couple of miles outside Kinlochbervie. It was a calm night but there was a big Atlantic swell coming in. The boat got stuck on the rocks and the swell meant nobody could get rescue boats anywhere near it. The Rescue Control Centre (RCC), which at that time was at Pitreavie, near Dunfermline, was informed and a search and rescue helicopter was scrambled from RAF Lossiemouth. Local boats were alerted but they couldn't get near. They would have been swamped. Being midwinter, the rescue helicopter couldn't fly direct to the scene because of icing problems and it had to fly round the coast.

Obviously, that meant it took a heck of a lot more time to get to the rescue. Meanwhile, the Bon Ami crew were freezing to death, one after the other. Unfortunately, by the time the helicopter got there, the last crewman had fallen off the mast and into the water. Because of that tragedy, fishermen, politicians and campaigners realised that the two nearest bases with rescue helicopters – Prestwick and Lossiemouth – were just too far away. After a campaign by local politicians and fishing bodies, it was decided that a chopper should be based somewhere in the Western Isles, and Stornoway was the preferred option. This would fill a huge gap in the search and rescue network. It is sad to think that it took such a tragedy for a helicopter to be stationed in Stornoway.

CHAPTER 5

Everyone remembers their first day in their first job and aircrew are no different. On the 4th of April 1988 I boarded a Sikorsky rescue helicopter to gain experience and assist the winchman. The job was to look for a missing boat off Muck and I was just an extra pair of eyes in the back of the aircraft. We searched for about six to seven hours for this boat, which was never sighted. The boat and crew went down somewhere but were never found. A few days later we were on another job involving another fishing boat called Seabird from Eriskay, which was taking in water pretty fast. We had pumps on board the helicopter and I went down with winchman Gordon Davis to help pump the boat out. It was good experience for me and we got the boat back to Eriskay intact and returned to Stornoway with a couple of lobsters. Those were my first couple of rescue jobs aboard the helicopter. I wouldn't have wished my first one to be a tragedy but I didn't get to pick and choose.

People sometimes ask me how much I remember of my first job as a fully-fledged winchman without anyone else there to show me the way. That was on the 19th of June 1988, but it wasn't an actual rescue. It was a medivac (a medical evacuation) from South Uist to the Stornoway hospital. It happened at night and I was in bed when my bleeper went off. I remember thinking before I went to bed that this was my first night on my own as a winchman without anyone's help. Lying there, waiting and wondering, and a bit exhausted, I nodded off. Sure enough, my bleeper went off. I was up and out of bed like a scalded cat.

In those days, a Land Rover would come round and pick the crew up and I was picked up along with the engineers. We drove so fast that I began to think I would never make the airport. A big guy by the name of Larry Graves, yeah, that was the driver's name. We made it to the airport safely and it was a tremendous feeling, knowing that I was the winchman and the guy at the sharp end. My mind was racing, going over what I had to remember, what with the infra-red camera, the radio calls, the medical equipment and everything else I had been trained on.

Keen as mustard, I was like a teenager going to his first job after leaving school. It was only a medivac. We got to Daliburgh Hospital and I remember marching in there and asking to see the casualty and the doctor. It was just a normal transfer but I was so proud of myself that day.

Then, in 1989, a second Sikorsky S61 came into service in Stornoway. Its registration was G-BDII so it became affectionately known as Beady Eyes. Think about it. It was only in service for two or three months when it was called out to its last job. There was a missing man in his boat, somewhere near the island of Handa on the west coast of Sutherland. I wasn't there. The crew was: Captain John Blayden, co-pilot Mark Wilson, winch op Vic Carcass and Cy Rogers, the winchman. The conditions were dire with a lot of fog, so visibility was very poor. The pilots had severe problems. Although I don't know why it happened, the aircraft ended up in the sea.

The guys all got out of the aircraft quickly, apart from Cy Rogers, who was stuck in the back of the aircraft for quite some time before he was released by Vic, who swam round and managed to open the back emergency door. That's how everyone survived. It was a close shave for them all that night. And, of course, it was the end of Beady Eyes. Neither was I on board Mike Uniform on August 24th, 1997 when it was called to a rescue on Stac Polly in Wester Ross. They were trying to get an injured climber off a cliff face on the stack when apparently, the rotor blades were hit by rocks which were tumbling down the mountain and the helicopter had to make an emergency landing at the foot of the stack. About two feet of each rotor blade simply sheared off. Captain Alan Elphinstone did a fantastic job getting the machine down and it had shuddered violently as he fought to regain control. Somehow, it landed hard without causing injury to anyone, though the crew was badly shaken. Winchman Shiner Wright was still on the cliff face when it happened. Luckily, he wasn't attached to the wire at the time. Mike Uniform was taken away, underslung by an RAF Chinook, and repaired. It was then renamed Stac Polly and returned to duty in Stornoway.

In October 2000 we were called out in the middle of the night to a ship called the Elektron which was in difficulties out at St Kilda. Now that was a difficult job that just went on and on. A passenger ship, the Elektron also had a ramp for taking vehicles on board and was used for taking services like refuse lorries out to St Kilda. That night the crew: Captain John Macintyre, Captain Neil Stevenson, winch operator Mike Birley and myself, went off in a severe storm to answer the call for help. She had broken her moorings off the island and was being swept ashore with 16 souls on board. The village at St Kilda is not an easy place to land a helicopter at the best of times because of severe turbulence caused by the local geography. However, we managed to get in towards the Elektron with the helicopter bouncing all over the place, although it got so bad that we had to strap in as the violent manoeuvres would have done damage to anything, or anyone, who was not. When we finally arrived, I was winched down onto the deck and we set about rescuing the passengers and crew.

Massive waves were battering the side of the ship and coming over the top of us. In order to stay close to the vessel and keep visual reference with it, we were lowering the passengers onto the rocks above the tidemark. The shoreline was littered with dead seals, squashed by the boat and washed ashore by the storm. We managed to rescue all on board and get them onto dry land safely. The ship was high and dry and didn't suffer severe damage. But that wasn't the end of the story. A salvage crew from Smit-Lloyd arrived soon after. These people were some of the best salvage crews you could come across. Very professional guys. They carried out what repairs they could so that the Elektron would float again and was seaworthy. She was towed off on October 29th and she headed off into the Atlantic to a yard in Ireland for repairs.

However, what the salvors didn't realise was that they were sailing into an even bigger storm than the one which had actually taken the vessel down in the first place. About 50 to 100 miles west of Barra, and still under tow, the hurricane hit. They were in serious trouble. Once again we were summoned and headed out there, with sea conditions picking up all the time. It was daylight when we reached the ship and I remember thinking how on earth were we going to get onto the vessel in those conditions? When you are heading out to a rescue you have plenty of time to think and it's best not to look out the window at the sea. Just get on with it. We would normally come across a flat spot in a storm and I kept looking out there and thinking, how the hell would we find a flat spot here? Massive waves were rearing up to about 40 feet, with white water everywhere. Tab Hunter was winch op, John Bentley was captain and John Macintyre was co-pilot. Before we got to her, I remember Tab Hunter turning to me and saying, "Well, Chris, I am bloody glad I'm not the winchman today." Thanks.

All the gear was prepared long before our arrival and the hi-line was ready to go. I was looking out the window and the waves seemed to be getting bigger all the time. It really was a sight to behold. That big ship was leaping about all over the place, still under tow by a Russian tug. The mast was swinging about everywhere and the crew were all lined up on the starboard side of the vessel, but we wanted to get them to port. All kinds of frantic hand signals and gestures were made before they complied. Tab decided he was going to try and get me on the port quarter without the hi-line; I think after a couple of minutes dangling at the end of the wire it was decided that wasn't going to work as I was swinging all over the place. After getting myself sorted out again and the hi-line deployed to the ship's crew, it was time to rehook and get on with the job in hand. After 10 to 15 minutes holding onto the line, my arm was about to drop off but I managed to get a foot onto the guardrail of the ship. Tab was winching out to try and get me onto the deck but I just couldn't get down any further. He was winching out as fast as he could but the boat was sinking into the trough of a wave and when she got to the bottom she started rising up again. The winch wasn't fast enough and I was thrown over the guardrail. I was swung out, upside down and, with my lanky long legs flailing above me, dragged along the hull. I was slammed and battered along the whole side of the ship – maybe not the whole side but that's how it seemed to me then – and before I knew what had happened, I was up at the guardrail again and swinging back on board. Knowing I only had a second or two before the ship bucked again, I quickly unhooked and played out the hi-line.

That's the most dangerous part – getting on board. After I landed we began getting the guys off, which was extremely difficult because of the movement of the ship. We all had to hold onto something or be thrown along the deck – or even pitched over the side. Somehow, I managed to hold it all together, controlled the hi-line and sent the crewmen up in pairs until eventually there was just myself and the salvage master left on board. We went up together as a double, so there was no one then to control the hi-line and we swung and spun madly in the storm. Somehow, I had the presence of mind to get out my knife and cut the line in case it became wrapped around my neck. Now that would have been a problem. The relief on these guys' faces in the chopper was amazing. They had been desperate to get off the Elektron because the taut towing wire to the tug had begun to slice through the entire bow of the ship. It was also hitting the landing platform on the bow and had begun slicing through that, too. The crew were really concerned that the boat was going to be split open, flood and sink beneath them. There were several vehicles on the deck of the ship. A large refuse truck belonging to Western Isles Council had just somersaulted off the deck and into the foaming Atlantic, where I am sure it lies to this day. Wonder how they explained that one to the insurance company?

It wasn't just ships in trouble we were called to at sea. In November 2000, we got a scramble call from the coastguards to go to the Sound of Raasay, because of a reported helicopter in the drink. It was a Royal Navy Merlin, one of the new type of helicopters that the Navy had for use down at the British Underwater Testing & Evaluation Centre (BUTEC) range. When we got there we found it lying upside down in the water. What a shambolic mess – a £57 million helicopter upended, with its broken rotor blades scattered all around. We learned that the crew had been picked up and were on a support vessel in the Sound of Raasay. There were no fatalities although the skipper had sustained back injuries. We didn't know how seriously hurt he was but we were tasked to pick him up and take him back to hospital. The rest of the helicopter crew were picked up by an RAF Sea King from Lossiemouth.

We got a stretcher on board the support vessel and very gently put the captain of the helicopter into it. He was conscious throughout and we took him to the Western Isles Hospital in Stornoway. They were all very lucky guys indeed, to have survived a crash like that.

The entire fleet of military Merlins was grounded after it was established that there had been a fire on board before that chopper had crashed. Imagine that, about £2.5 billion worth of helicopters that no one was allowed to touch. It was later discovered that the helicopter had flown all the way from Culdrose in Cornwall to Skye with a brake failure. The rotor brake had overheated and caught fire which had caused the crash. No wonder. Even a wee mechanical problem can have awful consequences. That is also why your car's annual MOT is so important, I suppose. Just remember that if you live in Skye – you don't want to end up in the Sound of Raasay with your wheels in the air . . .

If things were quiet on a night shift we were allowed home, but we had to be ready to come in quickly so that we would be airborne within 45 minutes of any call. One night in March 2001, the pager went off and I arrived at base to be told the coastguards had received a Mayday call from a German-registered fishing vessel, the Hansa, about 200 miles to the southwest of Benbecula. The crew that night were Captain Clark Broad, Neil Stevenson, Smiler Grinney and myself, and off we went into the stormy night. On the way down, we heard coastguards say that, after the distress beacon was picked up by a satellite, the radio was dead. There was no word from her. A Canadian aircraft on exercise in the area reported seeing flares but had been unable to investigate. We topped up with fuel at Benbecula. And our long-range fuel tank – normally empty, but for a job like that, some 200 miles offshore – had to be filled right up to give us as much time and range as possible. The night was awful: strong, howling winds, and one hell of a sea state, driving rain. We didn't know what we were going to find when we got there. Complete loss of communication can often be a bad sign. It wasn't looking good – especially with the vessel being so far out.

Captain Broad told us that once we got to the reported position, we would only have 20 minutes before we would have to head back to dry land. Only 20 minutes? It didn't give us much scope. We were told that Royal Navy rescue helicopter 177, from HMS Gannet, was proceeding out that way as well. When we got there, I was on the infra-red camera, scanning all around in the desperate hope of picking up something. Within a few minutes I spotted what I thought was a liferaft. The canopy was up so it was difficult to see what was going on. Then I saw what I thought was a hotspot when someone opened the fabric, and there was a survivor looking out through the aperture. Great. I was hoping others would be inside too.

Huge seas were rolling in with force eight winds behind. The liferaft would disappear completely and then reappear on the crest of a wave. Clark wanted to go as low as possible to look for survivors but he had to be careful to avoid the monster waves. I reported what I had seen and the pilots homed in on the liferaft and eventually picked it up in the searchlights. Smiler opened the hatch at the front of the aircraft, the cargo door as it's called, and he got his own searchlight on the spot. Moving forward, I hooked myself onto the winchwire with my hi-line in place, and off I went. Smiler kept winching out and into the chaotic situation below. I shot past the liferaft a few times as a wave would pick it up and fling it into the next trough. When I'd get close, it would disappear again.

On maybe the third attempt, Smiler got me close and after bouncing off a couple of waves, as luck would have it, I flew straight through that aperture and into the liferaft. Actually, it wasn't luck. That was only achieved through pure skill and years of experience by Smiler. Unhooking myself quickly and feeding out the hi-line as the helicopter retreated, I was concerned I was going to lose it. Had I lost the hi-line then, it would have taken more time to send another down to the liferaft – time that we just didn't have.

When I came to the end of the line I just gripped it so that the helicopter actually dragged the liferaft, probably about 20 yards or so. Had I let go then, it would have been disaster. I hate to think what the outcome may have been. Once I got some slack, I checked to see what was going on inside the liferaft. It was just a desperate scene. There were nine guys, mostly half-dressed in immersion suits, soaking wet; some covered in vomit, some moaning, some silent, just staring straight ahead. They were obviously hypothermic although none appeared to be injured.

I beckoned for two to come forward to the aperture to get them into the rescue strops. One or two of them tried to move but they were paralysed with fear. Being foreign, there was a language problem and I had to take control of the situation fast. I initially assumed they knew that I was there to help them but in such a difficult situation you can't assume anything. They were in shock and nothing was registering with them. Those poor guys had to be actually manhandled into position to be rescued. Managing to get two of them to the aperture, I got my strops round them and radioed the crew to start winching straight away. They were plucked out of the canopy and up to the aircraft. The minutes were ticking by. That was only the first two up. It was going to be a very close call to get all those people into the aircraft in 20 minutes. In a situation like that, the minutes seem to tick by so fast. I was anxious and willing that winchwire to descend faster. Smiler could not have been any quicker but everything seemed to be taking longer than it should.

I managed to get another two guys in place, dragging them from the back of the liferaft to the aperture. The rough sea conditions were making it difficult to drag a man across the bucking liferaft because it was bobbing about 25 feet high on the crest of each wave. I couldn't keep my footing and was on my hands and knees most of the time, still trying to control the hi-line too. Mountains of water were hitting the raft which was awash with seawater; debris and rope everywhere. And vomit, oh yes, loads of vomit. It was, frankly, a hell of a situation we were in. Up went another two survivors and, eventually, we came to the last one. I held him so tight, even after the strops were in place, as you cannot relax until inside the belly of the machine.

"Winch in," I said, and up we went, with me cutting the hi-line as we shot from the liferaft. I said to myself, "Thank God for that."

Time had ticked by. As we were still being winched up, the helicopter swung round and began heading for Benbecula. Once we were settled I asked the captain how much time the rescue had taken.

"Too much," he said.

The rescue had taken more than 20 minutes, maybe about 25, and the wind was changing all the time. It was against us and I remember asking the captain for heat. The onboard heater was powered by aviation fuel and he put it on briefly before saying, "Sorry, I have to turn it off." I knew then that it was going to be touch and go for us to reach land. We tried to look after the guys on board, giving them whatever medical treatment we could. Basically, they needed warmth and reassurance. There were no physical injuries but some were deeply affected by shock.

Being hypothermic, they needed to be kept as warm as possible so I got a pile of blankets from the hold to try and get them as cosy as possible. I then had a word with the winch operator about my mounting concerns over the helicopter getting back in one piece. Smiler just smiled and nodded. Whether he was worried or not, he wasn't going to say as he was busy with his calculator and charts. We knew there was a Royal Navy aircraft somewhere out there but we had heard it had similar concerns about fuel. They too had come across a liferaft – with no one in it. They hadn't had to spend time winching anyone on board so they should be carrying more fuel than us.

Things were serious and all options were under discussion. Captain Broad was sharing his thoughts with us. He told us he was even considering putting the aircraft down on a container ship and had also thought of diverting to St Kilda. On the negative side, any of those options would have meant delays in getting the survivors to hospital and there were still people unaccounted for. He decided to keep heading back to Benbecula.

The survivors didn't know what was going on or how worried we were. They had enough to worry about. But we made it to Benbecula. Once we had the casualties out and into an ambulance, we shut down the helicopter. We all breathed a sigh of relief and I asked Neil Stephenson how much fuel was left.

He said, "We had almost five minutes of fuel left." We had used up most of the emergency reserve fuel. Another five minutes and we would have had to ditch. That sent a shiver down my spine.

Still, we had made it. After we got the poor souls, who were all either Spanish or Portuguese, sorted out and into hospital, we went to meet up with the RN crews for a debrief. Then, guess what? We had just refuelled when the coastguard called again to request we head back out to the same area as another survivor had been spotted in the water by one of the surveillance aircraft. The tea and biccies would have to wait. Off we went. However, the winds had changed. We were just a few miles out from Benbecula when we calculated how far it was to the casualty and how long it would take to get there, flying against that wind. We realised there wouldn't be sufficient fuel to get to him and come back again. He was a long way out, at 212 miles – even further away than the guys who had been in the liferaft. Simple arithmetic. It was an impossible task. It was pointless even setting off.

Reluctantly, we turned about and came back to Uist, informing the coastguards over the radio that the job could not be done by our aircraft in those winds. We were all gutted and appalled that we had had to leave someone to die. We paced about, feeling absolutely dreadful. Then good news came through. Because of the change in wind direction, an Irish chopper had been scrambled which would be able to pick up the casualty. They managed to find him, pick him up and fly, with the wind behind them, all the way from Ireland to Benbecula. The final survivor was reunited with his friends in hospital. Unfortunately, we later learned that six others didn't make it. Their bodies were recovered some time later. It was an awfully sad feeling not being able to save them all. In all, we plucked nine to safety. The Hansa herself, of course, had slipped under the waves and was never seen again.

There was a lot of press coverage for a multiple tragedy like that, of course. Before long though, things settled down and we put those events to the back of our minds as we got back to day-to-day missions and searches. The following year, all of us in the crew learned we were to get an award from Sikorsky, the makers of the helicopter. Sikorsky award the Sikorsky Winged S Award to crews of their aircraft who perform rescues in their aircraft.

The company's announcement to the media was this: 'The aircraft was having great difficulty holding a hover over the moving raft. At times, the winchman used his own brute strength to keep the raft from being blown away from the helicopter. Nine survivors were found in the raft; wet, cold and suffering from shock. Despite this, the winchman quickly and efficiently took charge of the mostly non-English-speaking group. He was able to continually strop and dispatch them clear, two at a time, into the aircraft from the wildly unstable and crowded platform.' That was a good feeling – proper recognition that we had done what we could.

Then, sometime in 2003, my postman gave me an envelope addressed to Chris Murray QGM. What was this all about? Someone had obviously made a mistake. When I opened it, there was a letter from London asking me to go and see a certain lady at her home in the capital – Her Majesty the Queen. I was to be awarded the Queen's Gallantry Medal for my part in the rescue of the Hansa crewmen. That was a huge shock. It was the first of many envelopes to come from Buckingham Palace; lots of high-ranking people sent me letters saying you're going to be honoured and congratulations, that sort of thing. I was impressed by the detail in the official citation from the palace which was a proper, if slightly technical, explanation of the challenge we had faced. The waves were so high they had affected the automatic systems that should have kept us airborne over the spot. Clark Broad and Neil Stephenson had to do that work themselves, which was a nightmare in those conditions. The citation, sent to me in the name of the Queen, read: 'The seas were so rough that the aircraft system could not cope and it continually uncoupled the auto-hover. Manual controls were instigated to keep the aircraft low enough but not so low as to be hit by the sea.'

I was not used to this sort of attention; I had been invited, nay, commanded, to go to Buckingham Palace to see the Queen. It was all pretty exciting – particularly when my daughter Layla heard about it. She was going to see the Queen but she was more interested, at the time, to see her horses, not the actual monarch herself. So the whole crew from the Hansa job went down to see her Maj on February 18, 2004. The other lads were also getting awards for bravery in the air. We stayed in the Jolly Saint Ermin's Hotel, just along the road from Buckingham Palace. Lovely place, and appropriately expensive, of course. We trooped along to the palace, all kitted out in our best uniforms. It was a great honour but, you know what? I was way out of my depth. Not being used to all the protocol, I felt a bit embarrassed actually. We were welcomed and shown into a room with lots of other people who were being given awards too. Layla and her mother

Christina were in the audience in the ballroom where the awards were to take place.

We were given guidance on what to do, how to speak to the Queen and all that sort of stuff. Lots of military types were milling around with swords clanking by their sides and scrambled egg all over their hats. Initially we were told we were going to be presented to Her Majesty one at a time but then some high-ranking guy came through and said, "Change of mind, we have to get this right." In the end it was decided we were to appear in front of Her Majesty as a group. This guy even wanted to make sure that we walked correctly.

"I'll do my best," I said, as I wondered if he too, had a load of lead shot in his backside.

We were briefed beforehand and told that the Queen would be wearing gloves; she would shake our hands and then pull away quickly to shake hands with the next person. I couldn't see what all the fuss was about but the time came and we all walked in together.

We bowed and the Queen came up for a chat. She was very friendly, pinned on our gongs, spoke to all of us and shook our hands. Most of what we had been told beforehand was nonsense. The Queen was not wearing gloves and was happy to press the Murray flesh, and everyone else's, with lingering, warm and friendly handshakes. And she was in no hurry. Quite the reverse, in fact. She went out of her way to put everyone at their ease. What struck me was how amazingly well-briefed she was. She knew all about the rescue; she knew exactly what had happened, who was rescued, and she understood the critical timing which almost cost her government a helicopter towards the end of the mission. You know what? She was fantastic.

After the formalities, off we marched and mingled with the other crews. I met up with my daughter and Christina and I remember Layla asking, "Right dad, where are the horses?" I told her we would go and see the horses in a wee while, once we had had some photos taken. We were coming down a magnificent stairway and my somewhat bored daughter suddenly had an idea. Before I could stop her, Layla had clambered onto the banister and was off, sliding all the way down. Wheee! Well, she got some disapproving looks that day. There were a lot of stuffed shirts who obviously thought it was outrageous and very bad form to enjoy yourself in Her Majesty's little townhouse. I couldn't be angry at Layla. To be honest, I thought it was funny – especially seeing the shock on the faces of some of the old codgers. Well, she was only a wee girl of nine at the time. Lighten up.

Having enjoyed her spin down the banister, we then took Layla out into the courtyard and there in front of us was a gleaming coach and horses. Of course, she wanted to climb onto one of these magnificent beasts and have a look in the coach but she wasn't allowed to do any of that. Layla was in a right sulk and only just managed a half-smile when I took her photo with the palace Beefeater. After all the nerves and tension of the ceremony, it was then time for a bit of a celebration. We had a great time mixing with the other people who had been given awards too. Some were a bit snooty but most were fine with us. Then off we went to a swanky restaurant and had a meal and quite a few celebratory drinks. The whole crew had a great time, courtesy of friends of our captain, Clark Broad. It was very nice of them and we thoroughly enjoyed it. Thank you, guys.

Then it was off home to the distant Hebrides the next day, as Chris Murray QGM. As I explained at the start of the book, my name is actually William I. Murray but nobody knows me as that. And written on the side of the medal is 'Chris Murray QGM'. That was my late father's name. I like to think if he had seen that he would have smiled.

Maybe this is the time to mention that I had already been in royal company a few years before this. I was at the same table as Prince Philip for lunch in Lews Castle College in Stornoway and the Queen was behind us at another table. The invite had come through from Comhairle nan Eilean Siar and I was quite surprised to be asked to have lunch with royalty. I had my dress uniform on that day but, I am glad to say, no hat. Eventually, everyone was led into the dining room and told where to sit. Prince Philip came in and was shown to the same table as me. There's something about the old boy I really like. He's a bit of a comedian and it's sad that so many people think he's an idiot because he puts his foot in it all the time. His every attempt at humour is analysed and taken terribly seriously when it is, in fact, just banter he uses to relieve the tension. Others at our table included Alasdair Morrison, our then Member of the Scottish Parliament, Mrs Murray, the head teacher of Stornoway Primary and her husband, and one or two others. Once the formalities and speeches were over and done with, we got down to the meal.

Alasdair introduced me to Prince Philip who said, "Oh, you must be with the coastguards." I said "Yes," and Alasdair explained that I worked on the search and rescue helicopter.

"Oh, good Lord, I know lots of people who work on rescue helicopters," he said, and we got chatting away about various rescues he had heard about. Now, of course, his own grandson, William, is a rescue helicopter pilot in the RAF.

At that time, suicide bombers were causing mayhem in various parts of the world. These bombers had all their explosives attached to themselves under their clothes. There was a policewoman on duty at the college that day and, nowadays, they carry so much equipment on them − pepper sprays, handcuffs and radios, as well as a bulletproof jacket; she looked a bit, er, bulky, without a doubt. A member of the royal party took one look at her, turned round and said to us, "Did you see that policewoman? She looked like a bloody suicide bomber with all the stuff she had on her."

Rumours began that the royal had said something outrageous and soon the journalists were asking if we heard anything. Everybody flatly denied it. My lips were sealed − at the time, which was about 10 years ago now. Do you think it's OK for me to confirm the truth of what was actually said after all this time? Oh dear, what have I done?

Animals often featured in the rescues I have taken part in. On March 27, 2002 we were called to rescue a trapped cow. The call had come from Roger Baillie, the coastguard sector officer on Skye. A cow called Kate was jammed in rocks in the tidal area at Plockton. She had given birth down there and was in a bit of a state. We were asked to put our heads together and work out how to get Kate out of her predicament. This was something I hadn't done before and I don't think the other guys had actually been involved in any cow rescues either. We had to find an 80-foot underslung wire strop. Then a strong lifting net and off we went. We had an STV crew on board that day − my friend, the cameraman Michael Skelly, and a female reporter from the mainland.

I was dropped off at Plockton with the cargo net and the strops, and I met up with Roger and his team. We weighed up the situation – poor old Kate was just lying there on the rocks. Wow, she was a big old cow, and we wondered whether we would even be able to lift her to get the net underneath her. We decided we would try to feed the strops under her back end. The 80-foot strop was attached to the underside of the helicopter and we did manage to lift Kate's hindquarters. We then placed part of the net under her hindquarters, lifted her front end and twisted the cargo net round so that it was underneath her body. This may sound simple but old Kate was a mighty weight and it probably took 45 minutes to get that far.

Kate was also getting panicky by then which made everything difficult. She had to be sedated at one point or she could have gone berserk and injured somebody. Then came the lift, once the net was securely round her. The helicopter came overhead with the long strop and we hooked her on. Up, up she slowly went. However, despite her jab, Kate was none too fond of flying and was ever so slightly petrified. That probably explains why, when she was about 10 feet directly above me in the gully, she had an uncontrollable urge to empty her bowels. There was nothing I could do to avoid it. Standing directly underneath her, this deluge of runny, smelly, brown stuff from above splattered onto just about every inch of me. The chopper lifted the now-lighter Kate away in the cargo net and dropped her in a field near the runway at Plockton. It was a successful animal rescue. Well done to everyone. A great, professional job, by a gallant crowd of people who are proud to achieve a good result because, through thick and thin, they will always work closely together as a team.

Aye, that'll be right. When it was all over, the chopper came back and picked me up. I had scraped off the worst of the mess. However, despite my best efforts to clean myself, the lads claimed I still ponged a bit. There was no sympathy; I was ordered into the rear of the aircraft, away from everyone else. I was just too stinky, they said, and I was making a mess of the recently-cleaned aircraft. Cheers, guys. What was that about always sticking together as a team?

There was another better known rescue involving a cow which almost turned into a tragedy. We were called to Skye because yet another cow was stuck in yet another gully. Livestock do get into these sort of difficulties from time to time. The incident was recorded for posterity because we had the media on board that day too. Cameraman, Michael Skelly, and the journalist, Iain X Maciver, were keen to get footage of day-to-day helicopter jobs for STV and we invited them to come with us because we thought airlifting a trapped cow might make an interesting feature. And it did – but not the way we planned it.

We got to Loch Eynort on the west side of the island, where the cow was stuck on a cliff and a lot of coastguards were already there, all dressed in their yellow jackets and lifejackets. I was dropped off with the cargo net and some strops and the chopper took off again to await further instructions to let the long strop down. I had a two-way radio with me to keep in touch. She was in a very small, tight area against the side of the cliff. Although it was easy to get to, the cow was in this sort of hollow and she had been kicking about so everything was covered in mud and muck. We were trying to carry out the same procedures as we had with the previous cow at Plockton but it wasn't that easy. This cow had also been sedated but this time the sedative was having no effect. A vet from Skye called Neal Stephenson, an Irishman, was doing his best to calm the cow but she was still very lively when I got there which did make it easier to shove the cargo net under her. The helicopter then came over and we had a gang of coastguards, with the vet and myself, holding the net in place. She was hooked on and the chopper got ready to take the strain while we tried to get the strop absolutely vertical to prevent any swing. Then, in all the kerfuffle, something unexpected and potentially lethal happened. The vet, while manoeuvering to get his footing had ended up on the outside of the cargo net, away from the other boys, and away from the cliff. When the helicopter took the strain, the net and its mooing cargo swung outwards. There was nothing for the vet to hang onto except the net and, for a second or two, he grabbed on for dear life – and up in the air he went, with the cow.

Realising he was just about to be lifted out to sea, Neal let go. By that time, though, he was out past the ledge where he had been standing and poor Neal went tumbling head over heels, all the way down the cliff face. It was horrific to watch. He bounced off rocks all the way down, plunging about 40 feet before he finally hit a large rock at the bottom and bounced off, straight into the sea. Everyone froze as they realised just what had just happened – except Michael Skelly who, being the cool professional that he is, had filmed the entire sequence of events and was now filming poor Neal floundering in the sea. The water was fast turning pink around him from a stream of blood pouring from a gash in his head. We feared the worst. We saw Neal's body come back to the surface but no one thought he could have survived that fall. The swirling sea was carrying his body back and fore in the swell – there must have been air in his jacket – and I thought I could see that he was conscious. There was nothing else for it. I ran down and jumped in after him. The swell wasn't helping but I managed to catch hold of him and drag him to the rocky shore.

By then, large waves were coming in and smashing us against the rocks. The boys on the shore managed to grab and drag Neal up onto the rocks. Poor Neal had a huge clump of skin hanging from his head and some nasty facial injuries too. But, when I gave him a quick check over, I was amazed that he had no broken arms or legs and was completely conscious. However, we still needed to get to get him to a hospital straight away. While all this action was happening by the cliff, the chopper was still hovering overhead – still with a dozy cow in a net swinging under it. The crew had to go and drop the cow off safely somewhere before they could do anything else. Once they had dropped it gently on grass, half a mile away, the cow just got up, shook herself and ran off. I requested an immediate return to lift the vet and myself.

We were taken up into the helicopter together. I was holding a large flap of skin in place on Neal's head, as best I could with a glove and a bit of a bandage. It was a bit like holding the comb-over of the man in the Hamlet TV commercial. Sorry, Neal, I shouldn't make light of your plight, but I knew it was important not to lose that piece of skin if he was to recover as soon as possible. Neal was conscious all the way into the aircraft and once there, I was helped to tend him by Iain X, who was still on board and who had seen everything from the observation window of the chopper. Iain even took photos from above, of me rescuing Neal from the sea. Neal, meanwhile, was reluctant to sit down because the poor man didn't want to mess up the helicopter with the blood that was still oozing out of him. That explains the kind of guy he is. As fast as we could, we got him to the Broadford Hospital in Skye where he was patched up and eventually transferred to Raigmore Hospital in Inverness. Neal had a number of stitches put in his head wound but I was very pleased to hear he made a full recovery. He is retired now and I am just relieved that everything worked out fine for him after that day so that he can enjoy his retirement.

Mr Skelly had initially been dropped off with me when we went down to see what we could do with the cow. So he got great footage of everything that happened from his vantage position near the cow. The incident was the main item on STV news that night. The TV company later sold it to an American TV company and it ended up being featured in a series about some of the most spectacular rescues in the world. You can probably still find it on YouTube.

One footnote to that rescue was that we had to get the vet to hospital so quickly we had no time to pick up the cameraman. Michael was left on the clifftop while the chopper went off to Broadford and then to Plockton for refuelling. He had no idea where he was or how long we would be. He started walking in what he thought was the right direction and eventually came across some people on quad bikes who had been helping out. When we came back in the chopper, we were focussed on looking for a solitary, tired and grumpy cameraman. We couldn't see him anywhere and then had to start a search for him. When I think of all the time and resource that went into finding Michael Skelly, all paid for by the taxpayer, I wonder why we bother with these media people! When we did eventually pick him up he did nothing but complain about how we had left him without telling him where we were going. Some people are never happy. Just joking!

And there was yet another cow rescue incident in July 2005 – also on Skye – again involving Neal the vet. That time it was a cow and a calf trapped in a tidal gully. On a rising tide they would have drowned so I was dropped on the top of the ravine where I met the farmer and Neal. The chopper buzzed off until I called it back. We had been told it would be a simple, straightforward rescue – it was anything but that – as often happens. It was even more dangerous than the previous one in which Neal the vet had been involved. Here he was again, still bearing the scars on his head from the cliff fall. We both thought, 'Here we go again.'

Neal explained the situation and that mother and calf looked quite peaceful in the gully. It was quite a clamber to get down and we saw that the gully opened out towards the cliffside. Out to sea, there was just a narrow gap, only wide enough for a cow to squeeze through. Not wide enough for a cow and a man to get through together. On our arrival the cow became very agitated, with her calf following her everywhere she went so Neal decided to try and sedate her. At the end of the gully was a cave which went a long way underground and the cow and the calf disappeared in there. The last thing I saw was Neal with his hypodermic syringe between his teeth, disappearing into the pitch blackness after them. 'Oh-oh,' I thought. 'This doesn't look good.'

After a while, I heard a commotion in the cave and out trotted the cow and calf, with Neal in hot pursuit. The cow seemed not a little agitated and was heading straight towards me. I scrambled back up those rocks as fast as I could. This was not a happy cow, and there was precious little I could do to console it. You can't just say "stop" to hundreds of pounds of solid muscle and bone charging at you. And it's not going to halt just because someone happens to be in the way. She thundered past me into the narrowing gully and, as she went through, her hoof wedged between two rocks and down she went. We didn't hesitate – Neal was straight in there with that big hypodermic. As she relaxed and became sleepy, we managed to get the net round her.

However, the whole process had taken quite a while. The tide was coming in and she was in the narrowest part of the gully and had to be gently manoeuvred out of that position. We had no option but to manhandle her – or is cowhandle a word? – into the net. That was exhausting – pushing a leg here, an udder there, a horn here, a tail there. Somehow, we managed to get her into the cargo net. I called the chopper and they lowered the 80-foot strop down. We were still in a closed-in area and when the chopper began taking the strain on the strop, it dislodged boulders at the top which crashed down into the gully. We got the cow lifted clear and Captain Tim Noble and his crew moved away and gingerly deposited her on the moor. That particular rescue took ages and gave us many anxious moments as the cow rampaged around the gully. We had to move out of her way, smartish, quite a few times. I take my hat off to Neal Stephenson again, for the passion he had working with animals. He worked hard to get the situation under control. We didn't forget the calf either. It, too, was lifted out but, because of his small size, was no problem.

That was a really dangerous situation in which we found ourselves and I know some readers may think it unreasonable to expect us to put ourselves in danger for the sake of a dumb animal. I have no strong views on this because I understand both it, and the contrary opinion. But I will say this. When you are working with powerful and heavy animals like fully-grown cattle, there are many risks involved that you just cannot plan for. That kind of animal rescue can test your mettle and, in my own view, can be just as risky to crews as rescues from ships at sea, in a storm.

CHAPTER 6

We were training one afternoon in November 2006 when we got a call from Stornoway Coastguard, telling us of an incident up past Cape Wrath, in the Pentland Firth, on a ship called FR8 Venture. She was an oil tanker and we were told there could be injuries. We had little information but heard from the Longhope lifeboat that they were roughly in the area of the Isle of Swona and had a doctor on board. A wave had come over the bow of the ship and several crew members had been badly injured. We requested to lift Dr Christine Bradshaw from the lifeboat to transfer her onto the FR8 Venture. There were 15-metre waves which was nothing compared to the middle of the firth where there was also a huge swell. The lifeboat crew couldn't stand up on the deck and were on their hands and knees holding onto the guardrail, so they couldn't help me with the hi-line which was wrapping itself around everything.

With a lot of difficulty I managed to get onto the lifeboat, and then I, too, was rolling all over the place. After Dr Bradshaw's medical gear was taken up, she crawled along the deck and we got her into a rescue strop and winched up. We found the FR8 Venture and I went down first. She was massive, at 42,000 tonnes, with the storm hitting her side-on, causing all kinds of turbulence to batter me as I tried to descend from the helicopter. With a gale of up to 70 knots and a hail shower coming through, which was so ferocious it blacked out all radio communications for a while, it wasn't easy on the wire. The winch op couldn't see much and had difficulty controlling it.

I eventually made it onto the ship and the medical equipment was winched down, followed by the lady doctor herself. She went to see the casualties and, on arrival in one cabin, found two guys stretched out on the floor. Dr Bradshaw said to me she thought they were T4, the code to indicate they were deceased. The crew then took us below to another cabin where a guy seemed to be badly injured. As the doctor was officially recording the deaths, I continued down to the person below, who was in a lot of pain with back injuries. We got him into a full body vacuum splint and set up an intravenous drip. He had to be immobilised and given attention for a head injury. Taking him off wasn't straightforward. The chopper had to go back to Wick to pick up more fuel and a ship's pilot before we could do anything more. When it returned, the casualty was made ready for winching while Dr Bradshaw was sent up to the helicopter and I followed as a double lift, with the casualty in the stretcher. It was then a dash to Aberdeen Royal Infirmary to get him into the care of the medics. The chopper had to track back around the north coast because of the freezing weather; it was safer to follow the coast round to avoid icing. We arrived back in the Pentland Firth only to be immediately diverted to Loch Eriboll where someone thought they had seen flares. This was a false alarm. That was definitely a long afternoon and evening. For our part in the rescue of the surviving crewman from the FR8 Venture, Dr Bradshaw and everyone in the Mike Uniform crew received a Letter of Congratulation from Admiral Sir Jock Slater, the chairman of the RNLI.

Weather conditions can change so quickly that even highly experienced mariners can be caught out. It happens regularly in north-west Scotland and there is no better example of this than the time, in November 2005, when the Stornoway-to-Ullapool freight ferry, Muirneag, got into difficulties. She'd left Ullapool during the night but conditions deteriorated dramatically to a violent storm, soon after. The storm was so bad that the ferry was completely unable to make a straight passage across the Minch. The ship ended up well off-course, about 35 nautical miles to the north of where she should have been. We were called out because a man had been injured on board. It was mayhem on board – the tie-downs for the lorries were snapping – and serious damage was being done to vehicles below decks. The passengers too, were being slammed all over the place. Anything that wasn't tied down was being smashed to bits. It was a case of holding on for dear life. Very scary.

A passenger called Steve Collins had suffered a nasty head injury and we were asked to winch him off. We came across the Muirneag, a big cargo ship, being tossed about in seas, the like of which I had not seen before in the Minch. I had to be hi-lined onto her. The crew took the rope and guided me on board as best they could but there was still a huge pendulum effect on the winch wire. I managed to land safely and went to see the injured lad, who was 22. Cars and lorries were being thrown about so much that I would have to winch him from the middle of the open car deck – the only place with enough space to get a chance of a clear escape in those winds. After dressing his wounds and making sure that he understood what was happening, I told him just to hang on to me as hard as he could because it was going to be a bumpy ride for the first 20 or 30 feet, going up towards the helicopter. It is best to explain these things to someone who knows nothing about the procedure because being plucked off a deck in bad weather is scary. If you explain what is likely to happen then this helps avoid the risk of a toilet accident on the way up. Just as well I had explained because the pick-up was fast and violent. The boat fell into a trough as I hooked on and one second we were on the deck, the next we were 30 feet up in the air. The boat swung across as we were lifting out of the car deck, narrowly missing the guardrail, I'm glad to say. On the way up to the helicopter, we started spinning round, caused by the turbulence coming from the ship. The hi-line began to coil itself around us which could have caused severe problems, but my hand was still free enough to reach my knife, strapped to my leg, and I cut the hi-line and recovered the lad safely to the helicopter and on to hospital.

We sometimes went off on a job only to end up doing another one as well. In January 2005, I was part of Captain Noble's crew when we were sent out to the Rockall area to pick up a Spanish fisherman with cardiac problems. It took us a long time to get there, being nearly 220 miles west of the Hebrides. We had to fill up our spare long-range tank at Benbecula for that one. We expected rough seas out there and we had some difficulty getting onto the vessel. But we did it. As we headed back, we heard of another SAR incident in the area: a fishing boat was missing. As we got closer to Uist, the radio reception got better and we realised the boat was sinking with two crew on board who were in desperate need of rescue. Our priority then was to drop the casualty off on Benbecula and refuel the aircraft to give us the range to continue with the new job. Everything went well and we took off again towards the reported area, off the east coast of Uist.

There was no sign of any surface vessel although I checked with the infra-red camera and we did see some flotsam. The fishery vessel Vigilant was also looking for them. With the aid of searchlights I spotted a liferaft with two survivors in it. Ian Copley lowered me on to the raft which was partially deflated. Getting each of them in a strop was difficult because the flimsy craft was just folding in on us. The two lads were in a state of high anxiety and my extra weight didn't help. Eventually, I got the strops onto them and the three of us were winched up together. They were lucky, they wouldn't have lasted much longer. Back on the aircraft, I realised one of the casualties was Murdan Murray of Stornoway, whose other boat, the Ulysses, we would also save from sinking, just a couple of years later.

It was on a wild night in January 2007 that we came across the Ulysses. We were tasked to go to the Cape Wrath area where she was taking in water. The conditions were dire, with heavy seas and a strong gale. Mike Uniform, the Sikorsky S61, was our chopper that night and we had two heavy-duty pumps on board. I was winched down with a great deal of difficulty in that gale and managed to get myself on board, but not without being unceremoniously dumped upside down on the deck. Frantically trying to unhook myself, the first face I saw was a little curly-haired guy called Angus Mackenzie. He is known as Beaky, from Gravir, on Lewis.

"Och, it's yourself, Chris. How are you tonight?" I heard him say, as if I was merely paying a courtesy call. Waves were coming over the side and crashing down on us. He was soaked all the way through but still had a damp roll-up stuck to his lip.

He was as cool and laidback as he is on Cromwell Street in downtown Stornoway. This was a real emergency and his boat was sinking fast. My adrenaline was pumping. I shouted to Beaky that we would have to lower pumps on board quickly.

"Ah well, that's fine then, yeah," he says.

He behaved as though it was a sunny day in summer and he was going for a stroll round the deck. But Beaky helped by doing whatever he could. There were other crew on board too; I think they were Filipinos who, given the atrocious conditions, also did a very good job helping us get the pumps on board. They were flying about everywhere, up in the air one minute and crashing off the deck the next. The boat was actually in grave danger but, once we got the pumps going, we stopped the ingress to a certain extent. Eventually, she started to stabilise and the water level dropped. I was trying to reassure the skipper while Beaky's answer to everything was a cool, "Och that's fine, Chris."

He seemed completely unconcerned about the situation, as though he had been in situations like this a thousand times and this was just a normal day's fishing for him. Everyone else looked seriously worried but Beaky was just smiling gently and getting on with his job. We got everything under control, daylight came and Thurso lifeboat was sent to take the Ulysses under tow to Scrabster. The job was a success and everyone heaved a sigh of relief. In more than 20 years on the end of that wire, I have seen many petrified people when I have landed on board vessels in imminent danger. Beaky is the absolute exception. I have never met anyone who was quite as cool as him.

I did also meet another fisherman who was very cool – in a very different way. We were told by the coastguards, one night back in September 1998, that a boat had been in Ullapool for some radio repairs and had set off back to Uist. The gentleman on board was Ian Johnson and his wife had reported that she hadn't heard from him for some time, she was becoming concerned. Ian had a small creel boat and it was a calm night. There wasn't anything obvious that could have gone wrong on a night like that but we began checking down the Minch. We didn't have a clue where to start but we knew the guy was sailing from Ullapool down towards Uist. We guessed that leaving Ullapool when he did, he was likely to be somewhere on a line from there.

I spotted a few boats in the Minch – they could be seen from miles away. I then saw a wee boat between Stornoway and the Shiants which seemed to be going round in circles. If there was someone on board, why was it going round in circles? This became clear as we neared the boat. Approximately 20 yards to the north of the boat, the infra-red camera found a hotspot in the water. We realised it was a body, probably the skipper's – and he seemed to be alive. Captain John Macintyre was at the controls and he said we were going to run in so as not to cover him in downwash from the rotors, hopefully I would catch hold of him before this happened. That was the plan. It didn't quite work out that way. I was winched down with my legs in the water and trawled towards the casualty. However, it being a flat calm night, the downwash got on top of us. Had there been a bit of wind, it would have been behind us but unfortunately, just as I was going to make a grab for Ian, he disappeared beneath the water.

He was almost within my grasp and he just slid down. He had been in the water for something like five hours and to lose him at that point was just unbelievable. Suddenly, he popped up again. This time I got a hold of him straight away and there was no way he was going to slip under again. I gripped him hard and held onto him. Getting the strops round him, I made sure everything was secure. Poor Ian was dressed in just t-shirt, jeans and trainers but he seemed fine. We got him into the chopper and wrapped him up and kept him warm. Obviously, he was cold but otherwise none the worse for his ordeal in the water. We discovered that he had actually fallen off the mast of the boat while trying to do some repairs to an aerial. When he fell in, the boat had continued on without him and after a short while had begun going round in circles. Initially it had gone quite a long way away from him but had then started circling back towards him after a couple of hours.

Although the boat had been beside him, he hadn't been able to climb on to it as it was still whizzing round. The danger then was that he could be rammed by the boat. When you think about it, Ian was in a hell of a situation. He could have drowned, he could have been rammed, he could have been caught in the propellers and there was nothing that he could have done about it. He was obviously a strong swimmer, and a survivor, because not many people would have lasted in the water for that length of time. We got him to hospital in Stornoway and his family were informed. His wife came up to Stornoway and Ian discharged himself the next day, none the worse for his long ordeal in the water. There is no doubt that he was fortunate it was a calm night. Had it been a wild night in the Minch he would probably have drowned. The gods were with Ian that night.

I met him two or three years later at another SAR job in Uist and he remembered me from that night. Ian was a very modest kind of guy and he made no big deal about what had happened to him. He was very cool – certainly for those hours he spent in the water that night.

Severe weather can hit anytime and anywhere. I remember training in 1989 just outside Stornoway. There was no word of severe weather coming in and we had the winch hook attached to a grappling iron in the water, trawling for a target, or drumming, as we called it. I happened to look down to the south from the bubble window and could see what looked like serious storm clouds gathering in the Minch. Soon the sky turned an inky black. I brought this to the attention of the captain and chief pilot, Alan Elphinstone. He, too, had been watching through the corner of his eye and was a wee bit concerned. Nothing like this had been forecast. He asked the winch operator to haul in the grappling hook and as he was doing this, blue flashes were coming off it on to the water. That is a sign the air is highly charged with electricity. Having got the equipment secured, we found the wind had really picked up. The blackness had really descended on us by then and a storm was blowing in.

Alan said, "OK, lads. We'll get back to the hangar."

By the time we got the aircraft back to the airfield, the storm had hit Stornoway and the surrounding area and we were unable to land. It was so severe that we could see parts of the hangar roof and doors being ripped off. It was obvious we couldn't approach the area with the amount of debris flying about. The wind had picked up to about 80 miles per hour and we were concerned that if we came too close to the hangar, or any of the buildings on the airfield, then the helicopter might be hit. However, we didn't have to wait long before the coastguard got in touch saying three men had been seen clinging to a fish farm raft somewhere on the island of Great Bernera, off the west of Lewis. Luckily, we had a fair bit of fuel onboard.

The storm was now raging across the island and we would be heading straight into the path of the south-westerly wind. Our maximum ground speed on the way was only 20 knots. Flying across the moor, we saw it was completely white. Surface water from lochs in the area was being blown across the moor so that even the moor looked like a raging sea. It was an awesome sight. It took us a long time to get to Great Bernera but there was nothing we could do about that. We had just arrived when we were told that the guys had been swept ashore and they were safe. Time to head back.

We then got another call to say a man was adrift in his boat on Loch Leurbost. He was at anchor and had his engine on at full power but was still drifting out to sea. His engine was useless in that wind. We found him quickly and I was winched out by Steve Branley. The wind really hit me and I was knocked backwards and then swung a long way behind the tail of the helicopter – like a spider swinging at the end of its own silk, I was. This really shook me and knocked the breath out of me. The strength of the wind meant I could hardly breathe; my cheeks were flapping, my suit was flapping and I was flapping. All I could hear was a howling, screeching noise as the wind came through the winchwire. With the roar of the helicopter above me, it was an unbelievable sound and, I'm sure, a pretty unbelievable sight. The boat was somewhere beneath me in the white froth and Steve couldn't winch me straight down because I was such a long way behind the chopper. Must have looked really odd.

We couldn't use the hi-line in a situation like that. It would have been far too dangerous as it would probably have caught on the tail rotor. The casualty was doing his best to control the boat in the storm but it was still drifting out to sea and he could do nothing about it. Every time Steve put me down, I was just about on the boat and then, whoosh, I was blown over the side. Eventually, he got me on board after I was ducked in the water two or three times. He did well. It was a small craft, maybe 10 to 15 feet long. I immediately got the strop around the fisherman and we were off the boat and flying up and away. He was hanging on to me for dear life. We got him in the door of the helicopter and headed to the pier at Crossbost. The two of us were winched down again and a very relieved fisherman walked away with a sigh of relief.

Just back in the aircraft and getting my breath back, the next call came in saying there was concern about fish farm workers in Loch Shell. Their families couldn't get in touch with them. The turbulence around the sea lochs was really awesome. It was like mini-tornadoes coming out of the water. Alan Elphinstone had a hell of a job trying to control our huge aircraft. It was rattling and bumping all over the place and we had to be belted in because it was so rough. We were told to find a boat called The Houndback. We got alongside the cages and there was the boat, with no one to be seen on board. The cages were just being tossed all over the place. They were breaking loose and bits of wood were flying everywhere. Debris was floating in the water which was boiling white. We got in touch with RCC Kinloss on the radio as we couldn't get through to Stornoway Coastguard.

We reported that there was no sign of anyone on board or around the fish cages and headed back to the hangar to refuel. Later, we heard the guys had got into a small punt when the storm hit and had managed to get ashore safely. That was a great relief to everyone. When we returned, we headed back to the hangar because we had to refuel. Most of the debris had been blown away but the winds were still howling and very strong. Alan managed to land safely, a long way from the hangar. He told the crew to get out of the helicopter before he shut it down and the engineers refuelled it. He said that it was very dangerous to shut a helicopter down in high winds because as the blades slow down they can be bent by the wind. This is called blade sailing. So dangerous is it that the blades can, in strong winds, hit the helicopter itself or people within the rotor area.

Soon after the storm, local workmen were sent to patch up the hangar. While the work was going on, we were called in from home for a job and arrived down at the hangar. I don't know what made me look out of the window when the boys were on the phone to the coastguard but I did, and spotted flames shooting up from the roof. I called the cops and fire service and all these appliances with blue lights came screeching down as we were getting ready for take-off. There had been a hotspot on the felt, left by one of the workmen, which had been fanned by the wind and burst into flames. The boys managed to get the fire out without anything else in the hangar igniting – it was a close shave.

*

SAR crews have their own jargon although I am trying to avoid using it in this book, because I would like as many readers as possible to actually understand what I am talking about. However, here's a wee taster of some of the terms I used day in, day out. We were always involved in sweeps for mispers (missing persons) using the FLIR (forward-looking infra-red) camera and we were often responding to EPIRB (electronic position-indicating radio beacons) signals. When we gave the coastguards our situation reports, they were sitreps. Here's another one – medevac. That's a medical evacuation when the aircraft is used to transfer someone to hospital or between hospitals, usually in response to a request from medics. And, if the medevac involves a lady who is heavy with child, it is known to crews as a pregevac. We were involved with a lot of pregevacs in my time and they were often from a remote island involving mums-to-be who were facing problems, or potential problems, giving birth. Some were pretty ill when they were taken on board and were usually accompanied by a midwife or doctor – and sometimes a worried-looking dad.

One of the doctors we regularly saw on pregevacs was Dr Donald Duck, of Mallaig. That was his real name and he was well-used to hearing smart remarks about it. He even wore a Donald Duck badge on his jacket. A tremendous character, and I was so sorry to hear he had passed away a few years ago. He served the Outer Isles like Canna, Eigg, Muck and Rhum and all the other places in between. The good doctor always attended the pregevacs in that area and he was a lovely, helpful guy to work with. We had a lot of near misses where ladies almost gave birth on board but the first birth on board didn't actually happen until 1989. I wasn't on board that time but remember that she was a lady from North Uist who gave birth before they landed at the hospital in Stornoway. I am not sure what the birth certificate said about where the baby was born, but it was a time for celebration. Baby Kirsty will be in her twenties now. For some years after, the crew would give her a birthday present and, when she was 13, she was taken up for a flight on the helicopter with her parents.

Although the main function of a coastguard rescue helicopter is to help people at sea, the reality was that we got a lot of calls out to people in trouble on the hills, too. Sometimes we would be asked by RCC to go straight in and look at the situation before a mountain rescue team was put out there. The main thing was get the job done as soon as possible and to save lives without putting other people, or ourselves, in danger. The Cuillin Hills in Skye was a regular call for us. Another was An Teallach in Wester Ross. We were often down as far as Glencoe, the Cairngorms and anywhere we were required for a fast rescue. The RAF or RN had the main responsibility for these call-outs but we were called on to be available if they were busy elsewhere.

An Teallach in Wester Ross was a regular scene of rescues. It's an awesome hill, like a horseshoe, a ridge of mountains in a semi-circle with a deep loch at the bottom. It has very steep sides and is beautiful, but a dangerous place in certain conditions. A sharp ridge goes round it which people like to walk. One slip, or if they are blown off, more often than not, it's a fall to their death. That happened quite a bit in my time. Many a bloodstained body came out of that hole. We were tasked to go there once, when someone thought a walker had plunged off the ridge. It was daylight and we spotted two people in the gully. I was winched out about 300 feet above them and then scrambled down to where they were. One person was lying motionless and bloody while the other person had blood all over his hands and face. I asked the conscious person if he was injured and he said he wasn't hurt at all. The blood came from the other man he had gone to help after witnessing the accident.

Unfortunately the other person was obviously dead, or Tango 4, as we referred to fatalities. His rescuer had been trying to give him mouth-to-mouth resuscitation which was why he was covered in blood. He was OK but a bit shocked. I radioed up to the crew of the helicopter and told them what I had found. We couldn't pronounce somebody dead but it was obvious that he was. At the same time, the crew had noticed there was someone high up on a ridge, screaming and hysterical, whom I hadn't spotted. I asked the helicopter crew if they could move out of the way so we could get a decent view and listen for what might be another potential casualty. High up in the mountain I could see someone waving their arms and, in fact, making quite a racket. It was another climber in extreme difficulty and who needed rescuing – but quickly.

As the priority is always to help the living, I had to leave the other man in the stretcher (I couldn't do anything for him anyway), and go to this third person before it was too late. On the radio I told the crew what was going on and that we should try and get up to the ledge as soon as possible before we had another casualty. Quickly, I was winched up into the chopper. We closed in on the target and found a woman on a very narrow ledge, high up the cliffs. To this day, I really have no idea how she got down to that ledge. She was pretty hysterical.

Steve said, "Chris, you're going to have to be winched out many hundreds of feet above the ground – it's the only way we can do this."

So out I went and was lowered slowly towards the woman. I had a rescue strop ready as soon as my feet touched the ridge. It was dodgy because there was always the worry she would slip off, but I managed to secure her in a couple of seconds and soon we were back in the aircraft. We flew down to the mountain rescue base at Dundonnell where we found out that she was the partner of the guy who was in the stretcher. We didn't say anything about that and headed back up the mountain to finish the job. Soon after, a doctor pronounced the casualty deceased.

Some people think that public money shouldn't be used and that people like us should not have to put our lives at risk, rescuing people who are just maybe too foolhardy to understand the danger they are putting themselves in. The answer put forward by many people is that climbers and walkers should be insured if they are going to go up a mountain. That's a difficult one. I know in other countries climbers have to be insured but it is a difficult issue for the simple reason that: if people are insured, they will be rescued, but what about the ones who forget to renew their insurance or simply don't have any? If you have someone lying injured on a mountain and they are not insured, are you going to say, "Well, sorry, I am not going to rescue you because you aren't insured." Of course not.

I could not see myself having to make that decision. Many people have very strong views about those who get themselves into difficulties on the mountains, and some people are indeed guilty of stupidity when it comes to going on to the hills inappropriately dressed, often with inappropriate footwear. Some take young kids onto the mountains which is asking for trouble. The fact is, I think mistakes like that will be made regardless of what spotlight is put on people. Some walkers and climbers just don't think that there could ever be a problem. Such people simply aren't going to bother to insure themselves, and I really cannot envisage leaving those people behind if they are hurt. I just couldn't abandon someone. We are a civilised country, after all.

My view is that all mountain rescue teams in Scotland are of the same opinion as me on this. At this stage, I should mention the MRT boys and girls as they are true professionals, and the saviours of so many who would not be alive, if it was not for their unselfish, and unpaid, rescue work. They turn out all year round when conditions would take even the best of us to the limit. They are a hardy bunch of people who also know how to enjoy themselves. I take my helmet off to them. Right, that's me off my high horse about insurance. No more.

How can you lose a helicopter? We did once – but not our own . . . There was a job on the 19th of June, 1994, when a report came in that a PLM helicopter had gone missing en-route to Inverness. It hadn't reached its destination and we were tasked to check out the track from A to B. We spent a long time looking for this helicopter and were receiving constant updates from the rescue coordination centre at RAF Kinloss. We searched for about two and a half hours until we had to return to base for fuel, and by this time a lot of people were becoming concerned. We checked every possibility; the sea lochs, the hills, every nook and cranny. I was dropped off at various locations to speak to people, to ask if they had by any chance seen or heard a helicopter. Eventually, we flew over Kylesku and, lo and behold, there was the missing chopper sitting next to the car-park of the hotel there. It transpired there had been communication problems between the pilot and a group of people who were waiting for him at Dalcross. We found the pilot in the hotel, quite the thing, having dinner with his passengers, quite oblivious to the fact that the emergency services were scouring the north of Scotland for them. Not to worry – it was a good outcome – everyone was safe and well, although perhaps slightly embarrassed.

Divers were another cause of regular call-outs. The usual problems were difficulties with 'the bends', embolisms, and all sorts. A lot of untrained divers come to Scotland because of the water clarity and the interesting sealife here, and they are liable to get into bother. We would usually fly them to Dunstaffnage, near Oban, where there is a hyperbaric unit: a decompression chamber. Often we cannulated them and, if they were conscious, we gave them water to drink and put them on oxygen. That is all part of the treatment. We would fly low and as fast as possible to get them to safety as quickly as possible.

There was a sad incident some years ago, involving a friend of mine, a guy called Robin Swan. He lived in Stornoway and I used to dive with him for shellfish. We were called one day to a diver who was ill on the shore near Rodel in South Harris. The man had serious decompression problems. Vic Carcass was the other crewman and, while on the way, I remember discussing with him who the diver might be. Vic was an ex-diver also and Robin Swan's name was mentioned as the possible casualty. They winched me down to a boat on the shore where the diver was lying unconscious. It was Robin. We got him onto the stretcher, made sure his airway was clear, winched him into the chopper and off we went, down to Dunstaffnage. He was in a critical condition and we did what we could for him but later they had to take him to another unit in Aberdeen. He was picked up by an RAF helicopter but, unfortunately, poor Robin didn't make it to the chamber. We did have quite a few of these tragedies in my time. Deaths were something we had to deal with on a regular basis but when it is someone who is well known to you, it is always especially difficult.

It's not often that a vessel disappears without trace and simply cannot be found. In October 1991, a Spanish fishing boat called Frank C was about 300 miles out west of Lewis when she went down in a storm. This was actually outside our search area but we were tasked, with coastguards in the back of the aircraft as observers, to go out and check if we could find any survivors on a liferaft – or anything. There was nothing to be found. There were RAF Nimrods out there and they hadn't come across anything either. There are usually bits of flotsam in the ocean after any sinking but there was nothing to indicate that a boat had actually gone down. The searches went on for several days and came up with nothing. It was a mystery.

A few days later, we were tasked to go and pick up a rescued survivor from a large cargo vessel. The crew on the cargo vessel had spotted a liferaft in the Atlantic and lowered one of their small boats to have a look. They found a survivor from the Frank C. Just one – the 15 others didn't make it. He was a very young guy and a very lucky one at that. Some time later a body was washed up at Horgabost, on the west of the Isle of Harris, and it was thought that this may have been one of the crew who had lost their lives. From time to time boats do completely disappear like that. If they are way out in the Atlantic the crew has little chance unless they get into a liferaft. Even then, the chances of a successful rescue aren't too good.

Of course, we also had a few rescues that were just in the nick of time. We were scrambled from Stornoway to go up to the Kyle of Tongue in north-west Sutherland, in May 1993, to a man who had fallen out of a dinghy. He was reported to be in dire straits. As it's a long way from Stornoway to the Kyle, we went in as straight a line as we could in the Sikorsky. When we got there the dinghy was empty and there were people on the shore pointing to something in the water. It was the casualty. He had been in the water for some time and with the strong currents in the Kyle, he was going under and popping back to the surface. He was vomiting water and, yes, he was clearly drowning. I was winched out before we reached him and I was ready with the strops as we knew time was of the essence.

Everyone was prepared. I was trailed through the water and I was just approaching the guy when he slipped under the water again. He resurfaced, gasping and vomiting. I got a hold of him and kept his head above the water until I got a strop round him. He was close to death and he knew it, and somehow found the strength to hang on to me like grim death. Another couple of seconds and the guy would almost certainly have been a goner. It was touch-and-go, it really was. We got him to Thurso where an ambulance crew was waiting for him. I look back at that one and think to myself that just a few seconds can make the difference between life and death.

We have also had calls to, er, unidentified airborne craft. I am afraid that some of these calls came from people who had taken copious quantities of unidentified booze and who were almost airborne themselves, but many also were well-intended. Do I believe in UFOs?

No way. Well, sometimes. Maybe.

In October 1996 I was on shift with Roger Asbey, George Shepherd and Vic Carcass when we responded to a coastguard call saying an unidentified flying object of some sort had been seen somewhere over Ness, in the north of Lewis. Shortly after that, some kind of explosion was reported out in the Atlantic. There was all manner of unofficial speculation that it might have been a passenger jet. Whoa, this could be a big job. A gentleman from Ness reported he had seen an aircraft of some sort flying over with smoke trailing from it, and soon afterwards he had heard the explosion. The usual questions were asked – whether any aircraft were in the area at the time or were any missing from anywhere else? None were unaccounted for. We searched and searched but found nothing, only the usual debris that you find in the sea like ropes, nets, and so on. RAF Nimrods were soon scrambled and before long every man and his dog was trying to trace the cause of the blast. It went on for a few days but ultimately nothing was found.

The sightings on that occasion appeared to be genuine enough and were confirmed by a number of people, and the explosion was heard by a lot of people in Ness. They were sober too – well, mostly. Some thought it may have been a practice drone of some sort but the military denied they had any such drones in the area. As for little green men, I don't know about that. There was definitely something fishy about the whole tale anyway. Many people are still scratching their heads about it to this day. A poster with a picture of a UFO was sent to us from someone and was on the wall of our secretary's office for many years after that, to remind us of that particular enduring mystery. All those people definitely saw something. They couldn't all have been tippling in Ness that night. Could they?

Some people misunderstand me a lot of the time, but I suppose that's the Dornoch accent for you. There was one occasion when we were tasked to go to a place in north-west Sutherland. A lad on holiday had been creel-fishing by hand from the shore. The sea conditions were pretty atrocious at the time and he had disappeared. A lot of searchers were already hard at work when we got there. A large swell was coming in and you couldn't see beneath the surface because everything was white foam. We searched all around the coast and out to sea, but found nothing. One large rock, which was constantly engulfed by waves, had ropes hanging over it. There was a suggestion that perhaps, if the young man was launching creels, he may have become tangled in the ropes and dragged into the sea.

I went down to the rock. It was a long, hard job doing this, trying to keep my balance while still attached to the winch wire because I could have been washed off the rock myself at any minute. There were a lot of people watching what was going on as I lifted as many of the creel ropes as I could. One person in particular, at the side of the cliff, seemed very agitated about what I was doing and I wasn't sure why. We did what we could but didn't find a body. We continued the search until we had to return to Stornoway to refuel. Just before we left, I was winched down to speak to some of the ground search crews. They told me that the man on the cliff had been hysterical because he had spotted me trying to lift the creels up and thought I was more interested in trying to find lobsters. There I was, risking my life to try and find the body of this missing boy and this man was convinced I was trying to nick his lobsters! He was told by the ground crews about my intentions and did eventually understand and cool down. I reckon that must probably be the time when I have been most misunderstood. It was a sad end to that story because, sometime later, the creel fisherman's body was found in the area.

We were also called out to a foreign vessel, the Ana-Antxine, which was fishing west off St Kilda. The coastguard told us one, or maybe two fishermen had gone over the side and the crew were trying to recover them. I was winched on board and when I asked where the casualties were, was told, in broken English, that one was in the shower and he wasn't very well. I asked about the second casualty and they didn't want to talk about him so I assumed the worst had already happened. Anyway, I was directed into a shower room and there was this 18 or 19-stone man in a pair of underpants and he was as red as a lobster. He was in a running, hot shower and the crew said they had recovered him from the sea. How long had he had been in the sea? He had been under the water for about 20 minutes. It was obvious, if he had been under the water for that period of time, that he wasn't alive. He didn't seem to be alive although there was plenty of colour in him, but that was only because of the hot shower. It was just the wrong thing to do. If the guy hadn't been dead by the time they had put him in the shower, doing that to him probably would have killed him. There were also blankets placed over his legs. When I asked why this was, no one wanted to talk about that either. I removed the blankets anyway and there were large gashes in his legs. I understood then that he had been dragged over the side by the hooks of the lines. Perhaps that is what happened to the second person also.

My job was to get the crimson corpse off that ship and into the helicopter. As soon as I could, I began CPR – cardiopulmonary resuscitation, or heart massage – on the casualty, and continued this from the deck, all the way up into the helicopter. He was a very big man and we covered him with blankets in the helicopter and continued the CPR.

The winch operator, Jeff Todd, said, "Right Chris, you can do mouth-to-mouth and I'll do the heart compressions. Where's your pocket mask?" I didn't have it with me so he told me, "Right, just get on with it."

It was not a nice experience doing mouth-to-mouth without any protection because whatever this large gentleman had been eating earlier that night was coming up through his mouth. Garlic and all kinds of horrible stuff, but I had to continue the procedure all the way back to Stornoway. I now felt very ill myself but Jeff insisted that I continue mouth-to-mouth because we were not allowed to pronounce anybody dead. I kept up the kiss of life until we landed at the airport where a waiting doctor quickly pronounced the gentleman deceased.

I have to say I felt unwell for a long time afterwards. When Jeff came up to the crew room he said, "That'll teach you. You should always have a pocket mask and you should never do mouth-to-mouth without one." I don't think I ever did forget my mask after that. A hard lesson learned and another sad incident, that one, in August 1998.

The rescue services always have regular customers. These are vessels, usually fishing boats, where the crews, unfortunately, get themselves into bother now and again. We had a number of regulars, the Gem was one and Our Hazel was another. We were on Our Hazel a few times and on the Gem at least three times too. On one occasion I picked up an injured crewman from the Gem. Another time, she broke down and ended up against rocks on North Rona. The crew had climbed up to the top of the island and she was adrift below. We picked the crew up and took them back to Stornoway and the boat was then taken, under tow, to Kinlochbervie. She was patched up, the engines were repaired and she continued fishing after that. Then, in May 2001, we got a call to a fishing boat on fire. There was doubt at first exactly where she was.

The co-ordinates had been radioed somewhat hurriedly and were not clear. As fire took hold, the crew had abandoned ship and were in a liferaft. The position we were given by the coastguards was not where she actually was. Luckily, an RAF Nimrod was up at the north coast on exercise and they agreed to look around for us. They then saw smoke about 20 miles away from the position we had originally been given, and diverted us there. By the time we arrived the Gem was engulfed in flames and there was a large column of smoke billowing out of her. We found the crew in the liferaft and winched them aboard. Minutes later the Gem went down, just off the coast of North Rona, but thankfully all the boys were safe. Good job. We headed home.

CHAPTER 7

One lovely summer evening we were tasked by Stornoway Coastguard to head down to Glen Sligachan on Skye. A young girl had fallen and hurt her back whilst camping in the glen. She was one of a group participating in a Duke of Edinburgh Award Scheme project, trekking through the mountains. We used the infra-red camera to navigate through the glens and find the camp. After a while we found them near a loch. The boys dropped me off and one of the supervisors took me to see the injured young girl. The chopper buzzed off and landed about a mile away so that I could actually speak to people without it drowning out our conversation. It was very calm and late in the evening. Once the downdraught from the rotor blades had disappeared the atmosphere was absolutely still. Then the dreaded midgies appeared.

There were so many out there that their approach sounded like an awful high-pitched squeal in the dark. It was horrible; millions and millions of midgies descended on us. It was absolute agony. We were all being very badly bitten and when they're that bad no one can concentrate on anything. There was a bit of relief in the tent as I spoke to the young girl and examined her injury. She didn't appear too badly hurt but had to be checked by a doctor. There was a problem though. She was absolutely terrified because she didn't want to go in the helicopter. But we had a responsibility to get her out and get her professional medical attention. The young girl was having none of this and eventually she didn't even want me in the tent. Excuse me, madam, I'm trying to help you . . .

I had to go out and speak to the expedition supervisor. As soon as I did, the midgies began their onslaught again. Soon, the guys in the aircraft were on the radio asking why everything was taking so long. I explained that the casualty was very frightened and refusing to co-operate. By this time, I couldn't concentrate on what I was doing. I was scratching my face; the midgies were in my nose, in my hair and disappearing into my ears. I had to take off my 'bone dome', the winchman's helmet, to clear my ears and was then in an even worse state. I shouted into the radio, pleading with Captain Clark Broad and co-pilot Neil Stevenson to fly the helicopter over the camp. They wanted to know why. I explained it was an emergency because we needed to get these bloody midgies blown away. The sound of them laughing over the radio was not helping. We were really suffering.

This was really becoming quite serious; for some reason, the midgies seemed to attack me more than anyone else. They just go for some people more than others. The boys in the chopper eventually got airborne and hovered about 50 metres from the camp as they had to be careful not to blow the tents and equipment away. That did it. It was enough to blow the little blighters away and I asked them to stay where they were until I got the situation sorted out with the young girl.

Ah, bliss. Fresh air and no midgies. It made life so much easier during the 20 minutes to half an hour that we were free of the little blighters. After a while, the chopper landed near the side of the loch and winch operator Gerry Flannery came out and eventually persuaded the girl to come with us. There were conditions, of course. She would only come if her friend also came with her. Yes, yes – whatever. Let's go, ladies. Not too many people can say they have had the use of a multi-million pound anti-midge repellent device.

Midgie bites aside, various knocks and injuries have landed me in hospital a few times myself, but I remember one time, maybe around 2001, when I was on a training mission with the boys and had landed before teatime. Shortly after going to the crew room I began to feel really unwell. My hands, my legs and my face were swelling up in lumps. I had no idea what was happening to me and I really was feeling ill. It was obvious I had to go to hospital in Stornoway and they had to get someone else to replace me as winchman that night. There is no way I should have done this, feeling as ill as I was, but I drove myself to hospital. The doctor in A&E looked me over and it was established I had anaphylactic shock. I couldn't figure out how that had happened.

The doctor said "You've been eating shellfish, Mr Murray."

"No, I haven't eaten any shellfish at all."

He insisted I must be mistaken but I was just as sure that I wasn't. Luckily, it hadn't affected my tongue because I now know that what I had can kill a person very quickly. Anaphylactic shock is very disabling and I was given adrenalin to counteract the worst effects. Kept in hospital that night, I got better quickly and was back on shift the next day. I was fine and thought no more about it. The problem was that obviously, something had brought on the condition and I didn't know what it was.

The next day, the chief pilot made it clear to me that if this had happened, say, a couple of hundred miles offshore, we could have been in a serious situation. I could have died and no one had diagnosed what had caused it. There was a possibility this could happen again and it would not be a very good result for me if we were trying to find a casualty offshore and there was no able winchman to carry out the rescue if I became ill. I perfectly understood what he meant. My career could be at an end if we didn't find out what had caused the anaphylactic shock. I had never had it in my life before. It was just a one-off, surely? I saw my doctor and he persuaded the chief pilot that it was most likely a one-off. The chances of it happening again were very slight indeed, he reckoned.

I got away with that one and continued working until some months later when I was training with Dr Brian Michie and the crew. It was just a regular routine training exercise. We came off the helicopter and went to the crew room and, once again, I began to feel very unwell.

'Here we go again,' I thought, 'the same problem as before.' This time I actually felt ten times worse than I had the first time. Panic was setting in and I getting myself into a bit of a state. I told one of the crew members that I was feeling unwell and went to get some fresh air. Just in case, I told him to tell Brian Michie. I went out via the fire escape and I don't think I had even got to the bottom step when I collapsed in a heap. My skin was itching and swelling, my legs and face were swelling, I was just about to vomit and I could feel my tongue swelling in my mouth. I knew the consequences of a swollen tongue and that it could kill me. Brian Michie came down the steps and asked what was wrong. He took a close look at me and realised this attack was the same as my previous one, only much worse. It was anaphylactic shock again.

He got his drugs, injected me with adrenalin and called for an ambulance. The ambulance came within a matter of minutes; I was still lying on the ground outside, with blankets around me and I began to think I was about to shuffle off this mortal coil. Could this be the end – before I had had a chance to write my autobiography? The drugs Brian gave me certainly counteracted the shock and the ambulance crew took me off to hospital. On the way I tried not to think about dying but about what had caused it. I did remember that before I came on shift I had taken a Diclofenac tablet because I had some back pain. Having run out of my own Diclofenac I had taken one from Christina, my daughter's mother. However, hers were more powerful than my own prescription. I had taken them six hours before I collapsed. It also dawned on me that I had taken her Diclofenac before I had been taken ill previously. I told the ambulance crew about it because I was sure I hadn't eaten any shellfish or anything else which could have caused anaphylactic shock. My memory is vague but I think I then passed out in the ambulance, however the information was passed on to the doctors in the hospital. I was put onto a heart monitor and a drip, and given some other drugs. Before long I got better and was relieved to be told that I was indeed allergic to Diclofenac tablets and they had caused my severe reaction both times. Thankfully, this was discovered before I had taken another because, had I done so, it may have killed me. That was almost the end of my career, and my life. That's all behind me now and I have never touched Diclofenac again, bad back or no bad back.

You may have noticed me frequently referring to the hi-line. Basically, this is a rope which can vary from 150 feet to 200 feet in length and is used to guide a winchman, or even a pump, safely onto a boat. The hi-line is not the wire that carries the weight but the other one, which those on a vessel can pull to direct the winchman, or an object, into the target area. On one end of the line you have a karabiner, a clip for attaching one object to another. Climbers use them on the mountain as well. It's a quick spring clip, very strong. A batch of 5lb weights is carried on board the chopper, little bags filled with lead shot, and we attach as many of these as are required to weigh the hi-line down, depending on the wind. If it was a reasonably calm day then we would perhaps use one weight on the end of the line. If it was blowing a right hooley, we would attach maybe three, four or even five of them onto the end of the hi-line.

The hi-line is sent down before the winchman. It is clipped onto the winch hook and deployed down to the waiting vessel's crew or perhaps a mountain rescue team so they can control whatever is on the end of the wire – which will usually be a winchman, a pump or medical equipment. There is a handle on the end of the hi-line for the winchman to grab. The helicopter does not have to be positioned directly above wherever the transfer is taking place, which means that the pilot can get a better point of reference from the back end of a ship and the winchman can be winched up at an angle, to avoid obstructions. That way is safer for everyone involved and it also cuts out the swing, the pendulum effect, directly under the chopper, for the winchman getting on or off the vessel or side of a mountain. As soon as he gets onto the deck, he unclips himself from the hook, leaving the hi-line still loosely attached to the winch hook so that the winch operator can haul in the slack. The vessel's crew can still keep control of the wire itself until it's confirmed the winchman is ready to go back up.

All the crew has to do then, is pull the hi-line back in and the winchman attaches himself to the hook and off he goes. The crew on the deck will hopefully control the hi-line and how the winchman is lifted off the deck. In practice, crews sometimes have no idea what to do although the procedure should be taught in all nautical schools. They can hold it taut so that the line doesn't have a huge swing on. There is also what is called a 'weak link' on every hi-line. If the hi-line is caught on any part of the structure of the ship the weak link will break, rather than the hi-line snapping and causing a problem.

It's an occupational hazard getting wet from time to time when waves are crashing all around, but there was one memorable occasion

An Teallach – the place of many rescues and fatalities

Chris approaching a vessel on a rescue mission

Cliff Rescue Lewis, 2001

Rescue off Skye, FV Alex Watt, all crew safely winched off

INVESTITURE AT BUCKINGHAM PALACE

Chris, Christina and Layla at Buckingham Palace after Chris received the Queen's Gallantry Medal, 2004

Myself shaking hands with Her Majesty, February 2004

Sole Frank C Survivor

Rescue of Kate the Cow

Demo at Reef Beach, Uig Gala Day, 2009

My daughter Layla looking distinctly unimpressed by a Beefeater.
Buckingham Palace, 2004

Rescue from Royal Navy Merlin EH 101 helicopter, ditched after rotor brake failure, Inner Sound of Raasay

FV Gem on fire near North Rona, 4 persons rescued

S92 SAR helicopter in action

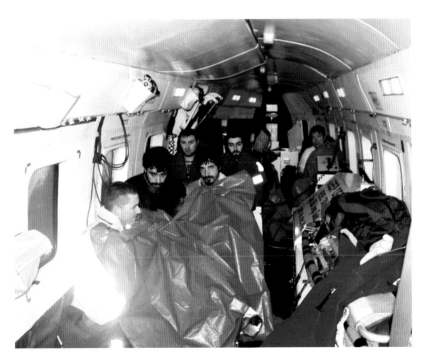

The nine survivors from the sinking of FV Hansa

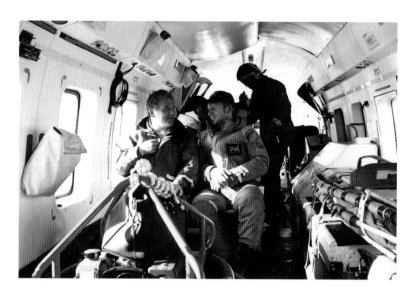

FV Gem crew

Rockall 2009. Our attempt to land with a group of Belgian radio hams – the weather had other plans!

The Cuillin Mountains of Skye where climbers often get into trouble

MV FR8 Venture in the Pentland Firth as described in the book,
November 2006

Chris on the end of the wire during another rescue

Rescue training on Ben Arkle, 1989

Return from Rockall with Captain Angus Smith at the helm, 2009

Our Sikorsky S92 Rescue Helicopter at base in Stornoway

Cuillins Rescue with Skye MRT, 2004

L-R: Capt. Neil Stevenson, myself, Winch Operator Smiler Grinney and Capt. Clarke Broad at Buckingham Palace after our awards

when I actually ended up in the sea and had to be rescued by my own helicopter. That was on April 16th, 1995, with the crew of Mike Roughton, Graham Findlay, Vic Carcass and myself. We were called to rescue a very ill Spaniard from a trawler, the Moraime. We took extra supplies of oxygen on board and went to Benbecula to top up our fuel tanks, then headed out west. It was a night flight out into the Atlantic and we met the Moraime about 180 miles out, with the help of an RAF Nimrod which had been scrambled to guide us to her and help with the radio communications. When we got there the sea conditions were pretty awful, with howling strong winds. Dr Brian Michie was with us because we had been told that the casualty needed immediate medical attention and if he wasn't taken off, there was a good chance he would die.

It was a really difficult job due to the significant movement of the vessel and the lack of references for the pilots because it was dark. Although I touched down a few times, I was unable to board. Circumstances dictated that we had to go to Benbecula to top up the fuel again so I was winched back up and we began the long transit back to Benbecula. I had noticed on the way out that my feet were feeling pretty sore and I couldn't understand why. My boots were getting tighter and tighter and this was becoming very awkward for me. I slackened off my bootlaces but foremost in my mind was getting this rescue done. I didn't realise at the time that I had picked up the wrong boots on the way out. I was wearing Tab Hunter's boots – he takes a size 8 and I take a size 10. Ouch, my poor tootsies.

We got to Benbecula and picked up extra fuel, then flew back to a position north of the vessel. Daylight was coming up which made it a bit easier for the pilot to get visual references, which just means seeing things around him which enable him to fly safely. He was able to see the horizon, which is always very important, and, of course, we were able to see the huge waves that were coming towards the boat which gave us a chance to pick a flat spot for a few seconds at least, just before the next wave came along. I somehow managed to get my feet onto the deck and quickly unhooked myself. Just as I did so, the boat reared up and a huge wave hit. The next thing I knew I was being catapulted through the air and down into the churning sea – right beside the thrashing propellers which were often well out of the water.

Oops. This was not supposed to happen. There I was, floundering in the water with the crew on board looking down at me in disbelief. I could almost hear them saying, "What the hell is he doing down there?" Because of the low light and the extreme conditions, it took a while for the helicopter crew to actually settle themselves and find me in the mountainous seas. They sent the hi-line down and I was able to catch a hold and pull it in until I got to the winch hook. I reconnected it and was plucked back out. I gathered in what I could of the hi-line and, without being hauled back into the helicopter, I managed to get back on board the Moraime to deal with the casualty. We got him on to the chopper where he was tended to by Dr Brian Michie and flown back to Stornoway, where it was confirmed that he had a perforated ulcer. He had various other injuries as well and there was a good chance he would have died, had he not been picked up by us. The trip had turned into an eight and a half hour rescue and, by the time we got back to Stornoway, I was in agony because of those tight boots. That pain will always stick in my mind. To add insult to injury, having my feet squeezed into Tab's boots for so long had mangled my toes. Just when I had recovered from the ordeal, a couple of my toenails fell off.

Communications are very important in the emergency services and I bet there will be some who are dying to know all about how we talked to each other on the chopper. There are various radio systems in use. Under normal circumstances, if not too far away from base, we would just talk on FM marine band radio to the coastguard in Stornoway on Channel 0. Depending on which base we were close to, for example, if we were up around the Pentland Firth or Cape Wrath areas, we would talk directly to Aberdeen, as that's inside their patch. If we were further north we would talk to Kirkwall Coastguard or, south of Ardnamurchan Point, we would be chatting to Clyde Coastguard.

We also had HF (high frequency) radio on board which, although not so clear, had a much longer range. We often used HF if we were going on a job far out at sea because normally, when we were out past St Kilda, we would lose communications with the coastguard on Channel 0 or 16, the usual calling channels for emergencies. So we would switch over to HF and no matter how far out we went into the Atlantic we were always in touch with the rescue co-ordination centre at RAF Kinloss, or the top cover Nimrod that would often follow us out. If we were doing mountain work in the glens and could not talk to the coastguard to give an 'operations normal' message, we would switch over to HF. When the job was finished, we would, say, sign off with RCC Kinloss and tell them that we were 'good two-way' with the coastguards.

Many a day we were very reassured by the RAF Nimrods coming with us on long jobs to provide top cover. These are large reconnaissance jets and were based at RAF Kinloss, which is now closed down and changing to Army use. The Nimrods were in the air when a major rescue was in progress. If we got a job out in the Atlantic, for anything further than around 120 miles it was usual to request a Nimrod for assistance with communications and to help us find the target vessel. That's top cover. The Nimrod crew would also speak with the vessel to establish exactly what the problem was and if there were any language barriers then these guys would often deal with that by calling up interpreters directly from the Nimrod. They would direct us straight to the casualty because time is of the essence on these jobs, obviously. The chopper could only fly for a certain amount of time because of fuel limitations so the sooner we got to the casualty on the vessel, the better. We would be in touch with the crew of the Nimrod, Rescue 11 for example, and receive information about the state of the casualty, whether it was a broken leg, an amputated hand or whatever, so that we could have all our equipment ready. We would establish if the vessel had turned about and was steaming in, usually to Stornoway or Benbecula. By the time we arrived, the vessel could be 180 miles or even 200 miles out which meant there was little time to spare.

Aside from using the Nimrods for communications, these big planes also carried liferafts and should a vessel go down, they could drop them to the surface. That could make a big difference to the outcome of a rescue – even before we got there. So we often did the job with a Nimrod circling overhead. We were visible on their radar at all times and when we were happy, and the casualty was on board, we would head back and, with maybe 100 miles or perhaps even 50 miles to go, the Nimrod would return to base in Kinloss. It was always possible that even a rescue helicopter like ours could ditch. Therefore, it was reassuring to know the Nimrod was around to do whatever they could to co-ordinate our rescue. On some occasions when we were far out in the Atlantic we actually heard the crew of the Nimrod talking to the skippers of tankers, asking what kind of weight their hatch covers could take in case we had an emergency and our chopper had to land on them. These guys really thought of everything. Normally, one or two on board spoke different languages which was a great help too. They did a fantastic job. There are no Nimrods flying now and no equivalent aircraft to take their place. That angers me but I had better not say too much.

Actually, why not? This is my book and I'm entitled to my opinion. The short-sighted decision by the government to scrap the Nimrod was utterly ridiculous. There is now no proper top cover for SAR helicopters. Lives will be lost, mark my words. Whatever defence cuts had to be made, this was one cut obviously taken by bean-counters, who perhaps know the value of money but who have demonstrated their complete ignorance about the value of human life. Right, that's that out of my system.

Before I go on, I should explain some of our other equipment. Zapleads are the popular term for static discharge leads. They are about 12 feet long and consist of a core of wire in a plastic or rubber covering. They discharge static electricity from the winchman, from the winchwire or whatever, to the sea or onto the ground, depending where he is working from. If he doesn't use such a lead and the winchman touches the deck of a ship on the way down, all the static build-up from the helicopter is going to pass through him – and quickly. There would then be a blue flash and a winchman could suffer a severe shock. The zapleads are normally coloured yellow and black to indicate that they should not be touched. Unfortunately, this often had the opposite effect. The lead would go down to the deck of a ship and there would be a fisherman trying to help you on board; the first thing he would see would be this yellow and black lead dangling down and he would think, 'Oh yes, this is a hi-line. I'll help and pull the winchman on board.'

I would be trying to warn him off but, no, he wanted to help. He would catch the lead and then – crack – he would be thrown on the deck in a big blue flash. That happened a lot and it scared them witless. They wouldn't do it a second time. It's just a fact of life that a winchman will get an electric shock sometimes, especially in rough weather when that lead is swinging all over the place. Sometimes I would hold the lead in my hand and throw it hard at the deck as I was going down. Some wire danglers will try that method but some won't – in case it doesn't work.

It's obviously a nasty experience for those involved but some days are worse than others – thunderstorms, for example. In that kind of weather it is pretty critical that the zaplead touches the deck or the water first of all, because it can really belt you if it is not discharged. People have been injured before and the effect of the shock has brought on health problems; I know of at least one winchman who has had to leave the service because of this. Every job has its occupational hazards.

In the past some clever clogs who think they know all about the latest avionics equipment have asked me, what was the most important piece of kit we had for navigation. The instrument systems? The comms? The direction finder? Nah. I would say the most important piece of kit is the pencil that the winch operator uses to plot on his map. That is one piece of kit we simply couldn't do without. Yes, we had GPS (Global Positioning System) on board for everyone, including the winch operator, to see on the screen in front of him. It works from a satellite, like a car satnav, and you just punch some buttons, put in a latitude and a longitude and once you have the speed and distance, it will come up with the direction of travel to take up, and an estimated time of arrival. A very smart piece of equipment if used correctly; it's used all the time on board aircraft but the guys also have maps, sliderules and the onboard computer as a backup. That's because anything that's electronic can – and will – go wrong, and usually at the worst time. That's why you have a backup and need a good knowledge of navigation.

I haven't mentioned the Polycon radio. That's the set used by the winchman. It is normally held in a little pouch on the winchman's lifejacket and has a lead which goes from there to his helmet. This way I could still talk or listen to whoever I wanted to in the chopper during a rescue. It's a really good radio system and we depended on it a lot.

The SAR team used to be asked to take part in carnivals, open days and even fancy barbeques, just like when I was a navy diver, back in the day. The coastguards would decide which ones they'd like us to attend. Sometimes it wasn't always possible, due to engineering work on the aircraft, but we would try and fit in as many as possible. It's good PR for the coastguard service. Demonstrations involved not just showing off the aircraft but also demonstrating how the aircraft worked in partnership with lifeboats, doing deck transfers, normally just 200 or 300 yards off the shore. If we were at Ullapool, for example, we would be back and fore, lifting people off the lifeboat, or if there was a demo further inland we would maybe use flares, hi-lines and make use of the coastguard rescue teams on the ground.

There would be orange flares billowing all over the shop and as long as there was plenty of noise and smoke it delighted the youngsters. Often we were invited to shut down the chopper and go off for dinner at a local hotel or perhaps even a barbeque. These are great community events and everyone really enjoys them. Occasionally, as part of a demonstration we would have a coastguard in the water and the winchman would zoom along, low across the water, pluck them out and drag them back to dry land. Everyone loved that sort of stuff. At times we'd be carrying out these demos when a call would come through from the coastguard and we would scramble to whatever rescue or medivac we were tasked to do. Of course that's a bit of a let-down for the crowd, but they always understood that real emergencies had to take priority. The same would apply to the lifeboat, they would sometimes be called away too, but that's the nature of search and rescue services.

We would also allow the public to come on board and they could have a look at what the big noisy whirlybird was all about and see what was carried on board. I loved doing that – especially showing the kids the big bag of teddies we carried in the back. That was always a big surprise. We carried these to comfort youngsters who were involved in rescues. It is amazing the effect a stuffed toy can have on a howling kid. Not just kids, either. We all need someone, or something, to hug when things go wrong. Even hairy-assed winchmen.

I have mentioned the various cows that have hitched a lift on the rescue helicopter and there have been other four-legged friends too. We often had dogs on board; normally they were from SARDA (the Search and Rescue Dogs Association). However, my own springer spaniel, Ben, somehow made it onto at least two, if not three, rescue missions. Ben was a regular at the Stornoway base and almost part of the crew down there. He knew what was going on and understood that if the scramble bell went off in the hangar then I was going away, perhaps for a long time, in the big red and white bird. Ben eventually figured out that if he went on board the aircraft he would be with me until it came back.

It wasn't obvious he'd boarded the first time round. We were scrambled and away we went; about 10 minutes into the flight I felt something nudging at my feet and it gave me quite a start. Under the seat, there was Ben looking at me. He had obviously hidden, because he had been caught on board before and unceremoniously booted off. I informed the pilot that he had five POB. That normally means 'persons on board' but this was four persons and a pooch.

He said, "What are you talking about?"

"Ben's on board."

He barked back – the pilot, not Ben – on the intercom, "Well, if he's on board he can stay on board".

This definitely happened at least twice, maybe three times. Ben knew what was going on and when the steps were down he would bolt up and hide away at the back of the aircraft.

I mentioned earlier that not all rescues have a happy ending and I remember one fatal air crash I was called to. On the 22nd of October, 2004, we were sent to look for a missing Highland Airways aircraft, with just the pilot on board. The plane had left Stornoway and was en-route to Inverness when it disappeared off the radar in the mountains between Ullapool and Inverness. We tried to follow its route, almost all of it over mountains, and flew all the way to the Dingwall side.

We found nothing, despite a long search, and returned to Stornoway for fuel. The RAF were involved too, in the Rescue 137 Sea King helicopter, and after refuelling I then went off with another crew under Captain John Bentley. We searched for another four and a half hours but found nothing. The next day, we searched again for five hours with no success either. We were also picking up mountain rescue teams and dropping them at various locations so that they could search too. The RAF were doing their bit; they had installed a bowser, a fuel tanker, near the Alltguish Hotel beside Loch Glascarnoch, for refuelling, which saved us all time. We refuelled there several times because we spent a long time on that search.

Many mountain rescue teams were sent out, including the team based at RAF Kinloss, and it wasn't until a few days later that one team came across some of the pilot's personal effects and, some time later, fragmented remains of his aircraft. There was no snow but the wreckage was so scattered it wasn't obvious to anybody what it was unless you were right there on the ground. The remains of the pilot were eventually found and we got the rescue teams back to their bases. Something had gone drastically wrong for the aircraft to have completely exploded like that.

Even now, I still do a lot of diving and back then, holidays from Bristow were a good chance to get the gear on. I remember one time, a cargo vessel called the Golf Star ended up on the rocks at Scalpay. The crew were taken off by the lifeboat and the helicopter, although I wasn't on shift. The wreck remained on the rocks at Scalpay for a long time. You can't see it now as it's rotted to bits but there was a huge problem with the hatch covers. They were being washed away into the Minch. Some sank and some ended up on the beach and were regarded as a danger to shipping.

I was asked if I would go and recover the hatch covers with a local diver called John Macleod, commonly known as Iosdaidh (which is pronounced something like Ee-yus-dee). We were to use my own 14-foot dinghy which had a 20-horse Yamaha outboard. We put it on top of the wagon and drove down to Tarbert where we met up with the late Donnie Morrison, or Donnie Agate, after the name of the boat he worked on. He was a longtime fisherman and a great guy. Donnie helped us with the hatch covers, dragging them off the beach and eventually we got them on a position on East Loch, Tarbert to have them hoisted onto the pier there. On arrival back in Stornoway I met up with another local character by the name of Michael Skelly, the STV cameraman I have mentioned earlier. He was a keen clam and lobster fisherman himself, and still is. We would head out around the island and dive for shellfish. Being interested in photography, as I still am now, of course, I had the video camera and I really enjoyed taking photos and filming under the water.

Life in Stornoway was enjoyable but it was not long before my wife Shona was transferred to Spean Bridge and I ended up travelling back and fore, when I had time off, to see her. That separation took its toll on both of us and some time after her transfer we divorced, I am sorry to say. However, that is what happened. We decided we had to go our separate ways. Then, in 1994, I met an local island girl, Christina Macdonald. The next year we discovered Christina was pregnant and in October, my daughter, Layla, was born.

That was the start of a new chapter in my life. I was a father now and the joys of parenthood and, of course, the responsibilities, started there and then. Layla was fantastic as a young kid and I really enjoyed being a father. I was completely delighted and the years that followed were the happiest times of my life. As Layla grew up, we took holidays in Dornoch. At first, we would stay with relatives or at the Trentham Hotel, owned by friends of mine. After a while we decided we would like to be a bit more independent so we began hiring a six-berth caravan beside the beach. It was like another home there. It was beautiful and we used to do all the things that a father and daughter would do. We had fantastic times in Dornoch and we still continue to do so now that Layla is now a teenager and all grown-up. I love her to bits.

Families are important to us all, whether we admit it or not. Just as family deaths affected me deeply in my younger days when I was diving, as I mentioned earlier in the book, they also affected me during my time as a winchman. There was a day in 1990 that I will never forget. I was training with the boys on the helicopter and as I came off the aircraft I was taken aside and told that my mother had passed away;

one of these dreadful events that everyone has in their lives. I spent some time back in Dornoch to bury my mother. It was a horrible time. Then, 10 years later, another shock when my older brother Donald collapsed and died in Dornoch. Another huge loss and again, I went over, this time to bury my brother. Life continued but it wasn't the same for a long time. Donald is sadly missed.

The fact is that deaths always affect crews, whether or not they involve their own families. I was on shift in January 2005 when we were asked to take some police officers down to South Uist because some people had been reported missing. We didn't know quite what had happened but realised once we got there that there had been a huge storm which had engulfed part of the coast there, and a family could not be found. It was a terrible tragedy for the islands as people came to terms with the fact that a whole family were missing, presumed drowned. The search lasted several days and involved ourselves, local people, coastguards and police. Our crew transported the coastguard and others around until the last body was found. It was an awful tragedy of the kind that, thankfully, is very rare.

Most of the time, when a rescue helicopter arrives, people are rather keen to be rescued, but not always. On one occasion some climbers were reported to be in difficulty but they told us they didn't want to be rescued and were really embarrassed about the helicopter being sent. This also happened at sea, occasionally. I remember one time we were called from home during a storm, to assist someone in trouble on some boat on the west side of the mainland. As we left Stornoway and were heading across, we saw flares being fired in front of us, probably about mid-Minch. This wasn't the person we were sent to assist but obviously, if there are flares going up, you have to investigate and see what you can do. We descended, put the searchlights on and came across a yacht. It was bobbing about, its mast ripped off, with the guy on board pretty anxious about the state of the boat and the possibility that it could capsize. I was winched out of the aircraft and managed to get my hand on the rail. As I did so, a static shock coursed through my body and I was thrown onto the deck before I managed to unhook myself. Lying there, in a pretty undignified position, I realised the yacht was in danger, with white water all around. I needed to get to whoever was on board as quickly as possible, to get them into a position for winching.

I spotted a fellow in the cabin but he wouldn't come out. He simply refused to come with me so I let go of the winch hook, much to the annoyance of Steve, because this meant the rescue was going to take up more of our precious time than usual. However, I had to deal with the casualties on board and I couldn't do two things at once. I could have tried but, with rigging being blown all over the place, the last thing I wanted was for the winch hook to get caught up on a mast. There turned out to be only one guy on board, a Norwegian. He was muttering to himself – never a good sign in the pub and much worse at sea. Eventually, I cajoled him into preparing for the helicopter transfer but he was still shaking his head and saying, "No, no helicopter. I want lifeboat, I want lifeboat." I thought, 'Oh no, here we go. This is one of those characters who values his boat more than he values his own life.'

Trying to explain to him that he had to be rescued immediately, I told him that by the time the lifeboat came it would be too late. My assessment was based on the sea conditions and the poor state his yacht was in. I really did believe the yacht could have gone over at any time. Besides, I was now very concerned for my own health and safety, too. However, try as I might, I couldn't persuade him to be winched off. I reported on the radio to the crew that, without doing something drastic, I wasn't going to get this guy up. I didn't want to drag him forcefully because that could have caused an injury. There was nothing for it; if he didn't want to be rescued there was little I could do. I could only tell the boys to pass the information to Stornoway lifeboat and the coastguard that the sailor was more concerned about his yacht. I told the boys to send the winchwire down again and I got back into the aircraft and we continued on to the first rescue we had been called out to, on the west side of the mainland, which had resolved itself before we got there. The lifeboat did eventually get to the yachtie and he was in a bit of a sorry state when they got him ashore.

We were also called to a dismasted yacht where the skipper refused to be rescued, on the 27th of February, 1999. That boat was the Taipan but since he was just outside Stornoway he came to no harm.

*

I don't think I have ever been desperately worried about the safety of a helicopter when I have been on one, although there was a wee jitter once, when we had to shut down the engine of the chopper because of mechanical failure. That was slightly disconcerting, I can tell you. It was the 30th of December, 1989, and we had been called to transfer a man with spinal injuries from Daliburgh on South Uist to Glasgow Royal Infirmary. The rescue went well and on the way back we had Dr Nigel Beresford with us.

Somewhere over the Inner Sound of Raasay, strange noises started coming from the aircraft. Captain Steve Colten told us he was shutting down one engine because there was a problem. When you hear the captain saying he is shutting down an engine you do think about what might happen and, yes, you do become concerned. Let me make this clear; there are two engines on the Sikorsky S61. If one engine is shut down, there is still another which can be used to get back to base. It is a normal practice procedure, shutting down one engine and flying with the other. That was done in training all the time. As we were in a normal transit flight there wasn't going to be any problem. However, when I told Dr Beresford that the engine was being shut down his eyes grew rather larger. An emergency call was made to air traffic control and all the emergency services turned out in Stornoway to greet us. Happily, we landed on the one engine without a problem.

We were called out to the Falls of Shin, near Lairg in Sutherland, in October 2000, where a young lad was missing. He had become separated from his parents at the roadside restaurant belonging to Mohammed Al Fayed, the Harrods owner. There's a fast flowing river in Falls of Shin and a thick wooded area with a lot of vegetation about the place. After the initial frantic search by the parents which came to nothing, the authorities were informed. It became apparent they needed mountain rescue teams, helicopters, police dog handlers and anybody who could help look for the wee fellow.

We flew in Mike Uniform and joined RAF Lossiemouth's Rescue 137 Sea King. We conducted a thorough search but because of the thick forest and shrubbery it was difficult to find heat spots. We could see some, but they were animals like deer, and dogs with their handlers. No sign of the lad. The police then asked the helicopters to skedaddle for a while so they could listen for any crying or any indication of where this little boy might be. Nothing. They then widened the search area right out to the extremities of the river. This all drew a blank and we had to head back to Stornoway for fuel. Some time later, as we were just about to return to the area with our fuel tanks full, we heard that a police dog handler had come across the boy under, I believe, the root of an upturned tree. Sound asleep. When they asked the lad, who was from Ardgay, outside Bonar Bridge, why he had disappeared, he said he had gone to chase the dinosaurs in the forest. He became known as the Dinosaur Boy and both local and national newspapers published pictures of dinosaurs with the story.

Not all jobs were so newsworthy but that did not mean they were not challenging. It was a bit breezy on April Fool's Day 1994 when the crew were called from home because one of the Army personnel was seriously ill on St Kilda. Stornoway GP, Dr Brian Michie, had been informed and when he had gathered all the information from the medics on St Kilda he thought it best to get the guy to hospital on the mainland because, as Brian said, there was a good chance he wouldn't make it if he was airlifted to Raigmore or Stornoway.

The problem was that the breezy day had become a severe night with thunderstorms, snow and hail showers. Captain Alan Findlay decided that, because this rescue was critical and the guy might not make it if there was a delay, we would go across to St Kilda and get the guy out. Under normal circumstances we would have waited until daylight. As soon as we were airborne it was decided that we were going to try and avoid the storm showers. I was going to have to use the infra-red camera as best I could and guide the pilot around them to get us to St Kilda without hitting any thunderstorms. However, some of them were so big it was impossible to avoid them. They were upon us before we knew where we were and there was extreme turbulence, with bolts of lightning coming down all over the place. It wasn't a very nice night at all, to be out in an aircraft or a boat, but we had to recover this guy. The thunderstorms worsened as we got 40 or 50 miles out towards St Kilda and the hail showers were just awesome – like big stones thumping the aircraft. When we arrived outside Village Bay, the turbulence really started shaking us up again. That bay is a windy place even in daylight. It is almost always a difficult place to get into because of the turbulence. At night in a thunderstorm, with lightning flashing around us and severe hail showers, it was a nightmare.

Alan Findlay did a tremendous job getting us into position for a run-in to the base itself and the landing spot on the island. He explained what he was going to do and said there was only one shot at it. Once we started going in towards the beach we were just going to have to continue until such time as we landed. Approaching Village Bay, it was apparent that we couldn't just make a straight run at it. The way the turbulence was buffeting us, we were going to have to crab in at an angle of nearly 45 degrees. In fact, we were pointed directly at a line of rocks called The Dragon's Teeth. As bolts of lightning streaked down they lit up the dragon's cavities and one of the crew members became very concerned that we were actually heading towards them. That's what it looked like. Actually, I could see on the infra-red camera that we were moving in towards the landing spot and Alan was, of course, fully aware of the situation. On the run-in itself the aircraft was shaking like hell; it was a big aircraft but it was being really shaken about in the turbulence. It took about four minutes to get from the side of Village Bay to the landing site and everyone breathed a sigh of relief when we alighted on terra firma at the landing pad. As we touched down, bolts of lightning and huge, golf-ball-sized hailstones danced around us.

We had to get the rotor blades tied down to the base of the helicopter otherwise they would be swinging all over the place. While we did this, Brian Michie got to the casualty and managed to stabilise him. He stayed with him all night. Alan decided the chopper would stay too, because it was too dangerous to try and get airborne again. What with high ground all around and such extreme weather, we would stay unless another critical situation occurred elsewhere. We returned to Stornoway in daylight and, best of all, the patient recovered.

CHAPTER 8

In all the years I was on the chopper in Stornoway, crew change was at 1pm. I would meet the outgoing winchman coming off shift and be briefed by him. He'd inform me about any SAR jobs, any training they had carried out and what equipment they had used. I needed to know if there had been any problem with the aircraft or any of the rescue gear, or if any items needed replacing on board – such as flares, for example. I would then go onto the aircraft and check everything myself. Even if I had been told everything was OK I would still make a physical check of all the gear – just a quick look at the medical gear, batteries and radios. If equipment was missing or unserviceable on a job then lives could be at stake. The pilots checked the aircraft all the time but the crews did also. That done, I'd be happy and go to the crewroom for a brew. The pilots would already have done their handover so we would sit down and have a brief discussion about our plans for the rest of the day. That could involve flight navigation or whatever. Engineers would also attend, sometimes there might be work they wanted done on the aircraft but, even if that was the case, we still aimed to be airborne within 15 minutes, if necessary.

We were called to a lot of jobs which turned out to be false alarms, albeit with good intent. Apart from actual hoaxes, and there were always some of those, there would be call-outs for flares. Most people think of red flares and emergencies, but often a red flare report turns out to be something else. Some people see shooting stars and think it's a distress flare. Anything that flies through the air, if it's bright, could be a flare and we had to take all flare reports seriously, at any time of the year. At

Halloween and Guy Fawkes particularly, there are a lot of call-outs for these unidentified flying objects. Some rockets can be seen up to 25 to 30 miles away, just like the larger kinds of emergency flares. Sunrises and sunsets can also be quite spectacular sometimes and, believe it or not, some people report red flares when all they are seeing is the sun going down. I have been involved in protracted searches where the only explanation could have been the glare at the horizon which can be really vivid. We've had call-outs for whales where people think it's an upturned boat. Flotsam can cause calls when people fear it's debris from a smashed-up boat. It could well be the real thing but we often just didn't know.

We've even been called to investigate when a jet broke the sound barrier. This happened on more than one occasion and we didn't know where to look but we had to go through the motions. We had calls for missing people who were often found having a pint of beer in the pub, who had not bothered to tell their own family where they were going. They may have had a fall-out and we found them sulking in their local. No matter, that's a good result and a happy ending. We even had a call to a boat that had a smoky funnel which someone thought was on fire. Lightning was also often mistaken for something more serious.

Once, a distress call came through about a ship, thought to be sinking, with a raging fire on board. We were told the crew were still on it and signalling for help. We were all psyched up for a fast rescue of the poor souls. It turned out the so-called ship was a lighthouse. The keeper was having a bonfire and we had to fly out a long way over to the mainland to discover that – yet another false alarm but with good intent. We even had a call from a concerned woman once, who reported someone shouting for help on a still day, up on the hills near Ullapool. After a short search we came upon a shepherd with fine vocal chords who told me he had been calling his dogs. I suppose "Shep! Shep!" could sound a bit like "Help! Help!"

The sea area around Stornoway covered by the coastguard helicopters is huge. Right at its edge is the Rockall area, an area we regularly flew over in the 22 years I was with SAR. However, until a few years ago, I'd never seen the rock itself in all that time. It just seemed that every time I'd been out there visibility was always too poor. Either that or we were there at night. Then, in May and June of 2009, a Stornoway-based yacht called the Elinca was chartered for a trip to Rockall. Aboard were five Belgian radio hams whose ambition it was to set up some kind of aluminium shelter on top of the rock and broadcast from there. They planned to broadcast for two days as that would be a record. It was their Mount Everest, so to speak. I had recently left the coastguard service and was invited along on the trip by Captain Angus Smith, the skipper of the Elinca. I had been on one trip with her prior to that, when we sailed from Oban to Stornoway, just to get a feel of the boat. It's a beautiful, steel 0-class boat with a 14-tonne keel, and has been round the world twice. She is a fine boat, skippered by Captain Smith and his son, Innes, both very professional sailors.

She has a tall mast, about 80 feet, and sails beautifully through any conditions. We sailed from Stornoway at the end of May, down through the Sound of Harris and out into the Atlantic, past St Kilda, and out towards the distant rock. We were lucky to have fine sailing weather all the way out and we each took watches. A two-hour stint – one on the lookout, one on the helm. They were a jovial bunch we had on board and everyone got on well, with a lot of banter. Belgians? Who'd have thought it? Everyone was looking forward to getting out there and setting foot on the iconic rock. Michael Skelly, that STV cameraman again, was on board with all his equipment. He was hoping to get on the rock too, to film the Belgian radio hams making history. That's him, always looking for a scoop. So desperate was I that I brought my diving equipment with me – just to be sure I made it on to the rock. If the weather was fine, I wanted to dive to the bottom of the rock, a depth of 24 metres. That was the idea – I mentioned this to my fellow diver, John Murdo Macleod, on the phone and he said, "If you're going to try that you'd better watch out for the sharks."

"What sharks?"

John said he'd been fishing out there for years and there were plenty of ferocious sharks that far out. I had been looking forward to the trip until I heard that. It puts you off a bit, to be told a big fish could come along and snap you up for lunch. Still, we were all looking forward to the adventure and hoping the weather would stay fine, way out west, so onwards we sailed.

We glided westwards through beautiful seas. Most of the Belgian boys were sick and in their bunks all the way out there. The weather wasn't that bad but they were confined to their cabins and feeling very sorry for themselves. We just laughed at them. These European types don't have the same constitutions as us Jocks. One of the Belgians was ex-special forces. His name was Theo Vanderydt and he insisted on coming up on deck and doing watches with myself, Michael, Innes and Angus. There was no holding this guy down. Whether he felt ill or not, Theo wasn't going to be shown up by anyone.

Eventually, one fine morning, we spotted the tiny speck that was Rockall, away in the distance. As we neared, however, the wind began to get up. A front was coming through from the south and although it wasn't expected until perhaps 24 hours later, we could see it was building and the sea was getting up. In fact, it was soon blowing a right hooley. The sea became so rough that we could only look at Rockall from a short distance away, take some pictures, shoot some videos and ponder what might have been. There was no chance of anyone setting foot on that seagull-stained lump of disputed volcanic rock. Not even I, with my mask and flippers, could try.

We felt very sorry for the Belgian team who had planned the trip for two or three years. They had spent a lot of money on the equipment and charter of the vessel and their hopes and dreams were dashed. It was just too perilous to even attempt to get anyone on to the rock. There was too big a swell. The final decision always lies with the skipper, of course, and Angus was emphatic. Far too dangerous, he said. If anyone had even tried putting a toe in the water, I think the very man would just have left us there.

I had to agree with him. Anyone looking at the weather and the swell could work it out. We could have been dashed to bits on the rocks. We sailed round the rock twice, just to say that we had, and I think we were all hoping we could hang around for a bit to see if the weather would calm down, but the front was already upon us. It was time to depart. And a very sombre ship's complement we were on the way back. Nobody said much, we were so bitterly disappointed. My diving gear remained dry in the box. The video camera remained in its box. It was still a bonus to me, though. I had actually seen Rockall with my own eyes.

As we sailed in, the weather continued to build up before calming down a little. Then it started again. By the time we were off the west side of Harris there was a big swell rolling in. We decided to spend the night in Loch Hamnaway, behind the island of Scarp. As we went in there the weather calmed down and it was a beautiful night. We anchored the Elinca in the bay, the yacht tender was launched and the Belgians, the crew, myself and Michael Skelly, took our cameras and went ashore. We had a walk along the beach and all said how good it felt to be back on terra firma. After about an hour the tender came back and picked us up to go back on to the Elinca where we had dinner, cooked by Innes, and then settled down for the night.

About 3am I was woken by the slap of the rigging hitting the mast and felt the boat starting to lurch about. I thought the weather was getting up a bit but didn't really think any more about it. By 5am, I was awake again and becoming slightly alarmed by the movement of the vessel. The weather seemed to have got a lot worse so I decided to get up and see what was happening. I got dressed and went up through the hatch to find Angus and Innes already on deck. We were being hit by what looked like the start of a storm, coming from the east this time. It was roaring up through the glens, down the sea loch and battering the yacht at anchor. However, the Elinca was coping fine and nobody was too concerned about it because a big ocean-going yacht like that is more than capable. After another hour though, the storm had grown in intensity and was screaming up the loch at about 70 or 80 knots. With the yacht at anchor, we were concerned it could drag and be taken on to the shoreline. There was nothing for it but to start the engine, pick up the anchor and run somewhere else for shelter. By this time there was little or no visibility. Just a white mist hitting us, with winds of 90 mph coming straight down the loch. The surface was being ripped off the sea and the severe storm was whipping up everything. The rigging was screeching and slapping against the mast. It was not a little frightening.

The tender at the stern of the boat was suddenly ripped off the water and became airborne. It was being flung around the mast – and the outboard engine was still attached to it. That was a serious accident waiting to happen. Angus shouted at me to get the knife to cut it loose and I grabbed the knife and hacked at the line until it parted. Whoosh! That was the last we saw of the dinghy and the engine. It went skiting off through the air and landed, well, goodness only knows where. Angus got the Elinca engine started and we tried to winch the anchor in. He had a hell of a job trying to hold the boat steady while we were doing that but, being the professional fellow that he is, he managed.

We reached another, more sheltered sea loch where we anchored an hour later. Ropes were then run onto the shore, in addition to dropping the anchor, to ensure the stability of the yacht. Everybody was relieved to be in the lee of the storm. Surviving what must have been hurricane-force winds had given us an appetite so Michael and I dived for scallops for our dinner. That was a treat but we collected so many that I think we were all sick of them by the time we were finished. We got bags and bags of scallops in that sea loch.

The following day we set off and headed up the west coast towards the Butt of Lewis, this time with a swell coming in from the west side, of about 10 to 15 feet. It was a beautiful sail though, and we went right up to the Old Hill, off Bosta on Great Bernera, and sailed close to the rocks there. That was a spectacular sight after the big disappointment of not making it onto Rockall. All in all, it was a fantastic trip. A time never to be forgotten.

Not long after, I had another trip on the Elinca. We had with us two Cambridge University students: Ben Sheppard, a fourth-year engineering student, and Robbie Howshall, a fourth-year signal processing student, who wanted to try out equipment they had invented. The plan was to sail to the Darwin Mounds, a coral formation about 80 miles north of the Butt of Lewis, and the equipment they had was basically a camera in a box of oil. I know this sounds rough and ready, but it was well thought out. Being set in oil, it didn't matter how deep the camera went, it wasn't going to be affected by pressure at depth in any way. Ben and Robbie wanted to take photographs of the sea life around the reefs and they believed they had worked out how to do it.

A bait basket was fitted under the camera to attract the wee fishies and other marine life to it, and the whole shebang was set in a flotation unit. OK, it was a bit more complicated than that but you get the drift. The weather was flat calm all the way out. The two guys were so excited to be able to try out their experimental gear and get the pictures from the camera. Unfortunately, when they put the camera over the side, there was a weak point which hadn't been anticipated. It snapped off and the whole lot had to be recovered and repairs quickly made. Skipper Angus managed to figure out a way to fix it, of course. He's probably a bit older than most fourth-year engineering students but this was no problem for him. He is actually a bit of an engineer and made a good job of it. The boys were really grateful; the camera was deployed again and down it went into the deep blue yonder, the spot marked by a big orange buoy. It was to be left there for 24 hours before recovery. We were all keeping our fingers crossed about the results on camera.

We steamed around for the next day and then made our way back to the position which had been fixed on the GPS. There was no sign of the buoy. We did see two foreign trawlers steaming away from the area and figured they must have snagged it in their trawls and dragged it off with them. We tried to contact the vessels on the radio but there was no response. They just steamed off over the horizon and that was the last we saw of them. You can imagine the guys' disappointment. Thousands of pounds worth of equipment and two years of investing and experimenting – using their own special knowledge to develop these devices – all lost in a few hours. The students were absolutely distraught by what had happened and we were all very pissed off as we sailed back to Stornoway, trying to console the lads and wishing them well for the future.

Not many people nowadays come into contact with lethal explosives. Having been in the bomb disposal service myself, it was a bit of a coincidence that I ended up having to call on my former colleagues for help, many years later. I often walked on the beach near Stornoway Airport, which is beautiful and secluded, before going on shift. I went there with my trusty hound, Ben the spaniel, every day from 11.30 to noon. Very often too, after a 24-hour shift, we would go down to that beach which is maybe a mile or so long, and have a good long walk.

Sometimes, I would take my daughter down there with me, too. Layla was five years old when, on July 11th, 2002, she said she wanted to go for a swim. Although it was July, there was a bitter wind blowing so we decided to go for a walk on the beach instead and we walked right round, past the far end of the runway on the Steinish side. Some time before, wild weather had washed sand away from the dunes and left a lot of bare bedrock. Scrap metal had been left lying around among the dunes – possibly from the military base which had been there during the war. The dog was running back and fore between us and we were throwing seashells for him to pick up. The dog picked up what I thought was a stone and was teasing Layla and me with it, wanting us to chase him. I noticed that the 'stone' looked like something else entirely. As I got closer to Ben I was shocked to see what he had in his mouth. It was a bloody grenade.

My mouth fell open. I recognised it straight away; I had blown up enough of them in my navy days. It was your actual Type 23 Mills Grenade from the Second World War: I could see the telltale chunks in the side of it, and rust around the area where the pin and handle should be. No doubt about it. My blood ran cold as the seriousness of the situation I was in began to slowly dawn on me. How on earth could I get it away from the dog? Wherever we went, Ben was going to chase us, taking this lethal bomb with him. Layla, of course, didn't understand my concerns. I asked her to stay where she was while I tried to get this thing off the dog but no, Layla wouldn't have it. She was going to stay with her daddy, come what may. Having seen and disposed of these devices before, in the navy, I knew the incredible damage they could do.

There was nothing else for it but to try and coax Ben to come to heel. Eventually, after what seemed like an eternity, I did manage to catch a hold of him. I got him by the scruff of the neck and prised the grenade ever so carefully out of his mouth. Please don't chew it like that, Ben . . .

I explained to Layla that this wasn't a nice thing, that it was a bomb which could kill people, and she just started laughing and chuckling, happily trying to grab this new toy. To a five-year-old, the grenade was just a new plaything. Placing it back in the sand, I got hold of my dog, grabbed my curious daughter with the other hand and with a great sigh of relief fled back to the sand dunes. From a safe distance away, I phoned the authorities. Soon the place was cordoned off by the police and coastguards and a mine disposal team from my old workplace at Faslane arrived and blew the thing up.

There may be some people who are unaware that there are roads in the sky that aircraft use. They are called airways and they are straight lines which most civil aircraft will always try to follow. In the case of rescue helicopters, roads called low-level routes are used. These generally follow roads and railway lines through the glens and our choppers used to follow them, for example, to get quickly and safely to Raigmore Hospital in Inverness during foul weather. If the weather was really snowy and icy, then we would have no choice but to fly right round the north of Scotland, by Cape Wrath, and track round to Raigmore or even, sometimes, Aberdeen. We would weigh up the situation very carefully, as casualties could be in urgent need of hospital attention, and we had to balance the safest route with medical urgency. Icing is one of the main dangers for helicopters. It can happen very quickly in cloud and is downright dangerous, although the new S92 helicopters have much more advanced anti-icing systems than the old S61. In situations where we flew into cloud, the chopper could freeze up quickly. In these conditions we would have to go up around the coast, over the sea where, in that salt-laden environment, there was less chance of a build-up of ice. It added hours to the job but safety came first.

We regularly had to make decisions about our route and I remember one time, while taking a casualty to Raigmore Hospital, when we decided that the safest and quickest option was to take the low-level route from Stornoway to Ullapool to Loch Glascarnoch, Garve and down to Dingwall and Inverness. Everything seemed pretty clear, we had checked the forecast and there were some pretty heavy showers going through from time to time but we reckoned that we would be able to make it. Unfortunately, when we reached the west end of Loch Glascarnoch, the snow really started to come down. It soon became a blizzard and got so bad that we had to land the helicopter in a layby at the east end of the loch. We had to wait until the snow eased off a bit before attempting to go any further. However, conditions just got worse.

Huge flakes began to build up a thick covering on the helicopter which was not a good thing. Any snow lying near the engines can be sucked in and cause serious problems. So Captain John Bentley decided the best option was to get the chopper out of there and continue on down the road.

It was a case of crawling along to make sure we were in contact with the road, using the Mark 1 Eyeball. Eh, I hear you say? That's an aviation and military term for the human eye, as opposed to electronic eyes like radars, etc. Our crawling along involved intense map-reading, making sure we knew exactly where we were all the time. We had to follow passing-place signs while avoiding all the electricity and telephone poles and wires. It was a long, laborious journey, often just hover-crawling, (that's not a proper technical term, but you know what I mean) following the edges of the road until we reached the Dingwall side. Thankfully, it cleared up a bit there and we managed to get to Raigmore Hospital safely with the casualty.

You will see there are quite a few photos in this book. Most of them are my own although I have been kindly allowed to include some taken by other people. My own interest in photography has been a bit of a boon for this book.

There was no way I could afford the best cameras like Canon, Olympus and Nikon, so I made do with a little pocket camera. It worked fine and I often took pictures wherever I happened to be. After I left the Royal Navy, and particularly when I started in search and rescue, I began buying cameras to record my life up in the air and down on land. Eventually, someone mentioned digital cameras to me and I knew this was a mysterious world that I had to explore. There were big advantages to them, as long as you had a computer, so that came next.

Once mastered, digital photography was easy, even for a cloth-ears like me. As time went on, my photos got better; the computer programmes got better and I could edit and enhance the pictures. As an old fogey, I classed this as cheating at first but I did a little bit of cheating here and there myself. Gone were the days when you had to get pictures developed at Angus Smith Photographic before you could see them. Eventually, I managed to take some rather nice pictures indeed. I was quite chuffed with them and began putting some in frames and in albums, just to enjoy them.

The Sun newspaper was running a competition and I had a couple of pictures, taken in a remote part of the South Lochs area of the Isle of Lewis, called Valamus. I had been in the area for a day with Kenny Alex Maclean, a former shepherd and stalker who had connections with the district. I decided to enter a picture of Kenny Alex standing with his walking stick and wearing his loud purple jumper, which his wife hated, (and still does), with a background of beautiful hills behind him. I think it was in August or September 2005 when I got a phone call from The Sun to say the picture I had submitted was going to be in their top 10 and it was to form part of an exhibition in the Dean Gallery in Edinburgh.

I was even invited to the gallery on the evening the winner was going to be picked. Somehow, I got time off and managed to get there. It was all very last-minute; I wangled leave at short notice and made it to Edinburgh but the organisers weren't actually expecting me. When I arrived, everyone was sipping champagne and scoffing those wee biscuits with a prawn or two on top of them. It was all a bit hoity-toity for me. Eventually, it was time for the prize-giving and there was a countdown of all the prize-winners. As the evening wore on, my name hadn't been mentioned and I was getting very anxious. Pah! I wasn't mentioned at all – simply because they hadn't expected me to be there.

First Minister Jack McConnell was there that night, along with Arthur Edwards, the famous royal reporter from The Sun, and a few of the great and the good. Aisling Friel, Miss Scotland 2005, was there and I had a good yarn with her. And a cuddle. That made my night. I even had my photograph taken with her but unfortunately they didn't give me a copy.

I entered another competition, too. This one wasn't really my doing, but my daughter Layla took a fancy to a photo I had taken of my current English Springer Spaniel, Rhonan. I took an evening shot of him at a loch in Stornoway with the water shooting off his tail, caught in the flash of the camera. It was a beautiful picture. Layla wanted to submit it to some animal photo competition and a phone call came again, to say it had got third prize. They sent us a framed picture of the dog in the water, sponsored by some pet food company, and it has pride of place in the house. These are the only two photography competitions I have gone in for but I dare say I might do a few more in the future.

To get back to operational matters, I am often asked if winchmen need to be trained as doctors or paramedics. The answer is yes and no. We are trained as paramedics because we do need to have enough knowledge to keep a patient alive, long enough to get them to hospital or to a doctor. Our medical training was always under review from the day I started in 1987. Initially we were given basic medical training in Aberdeen, but as time went on the training became more complex. When the new operator, CHC, took over the SAR contract, we were told we were going to have to ditch the medical training that we had previously done in Portsmouth over the years, and that the winchman especially, would have to go through a three-week course of intensive medical training at COSARM: the College of Search and Rescue Medicine at RAF St Mawgan in Cornwall.

The medical training we underwent at Portsmouth was very relevant and very important. There is a lot to learn, and I could probably write another book about that, so I won't go into detail. We trained on a regular basis on-site with Chris Gibbons, a winchman and paramedic instructor, and we often did this with dummies. No, I'm not talking about any of the aircrew here. I mean mannequins. The training was as near to the real thing as we could get. We had to know how to cannulate, (putting needles with drugs or tranquillisers into people), and how to intubate – inserting a plastic tube down the airway of a casualty who's unconscious. We always had to be ready to use basic life support, such as CPR and resuscitation, and there are defibrillators and blood pressure monitors on board all choppers. We were not doctors but the rear seat crew at the base are trained to paramedic standard and we were there to look after, and stabilise, any casualty until they were delivered safely to a hospital.

Sticking a needle in someone never made me feel squeamish because we were all trained for that; every two years the crew would go to Portsmouth for a couple of days in the classroom, going through medical scenarios and taking exams. That would be followed by a few days in a genuine hospital operating theatre. We were given placements where we had to carry out 20 or 30 cannulations on live casualties, mainly people who were in for minor operations. They all had to be cannulated to knock them out before going under the knife – done, of course, with their permission. It was our job to make sure the needles were inserted before the anaesthetist came along and pumped in the white stuff to knock them out. We were also expected to use screens to monitor the patients after they were unconscious. We had to keep tabs on their oxygen levels, blood pressure, heart rate and so on. We also applied airway management to these patients: inserting a plastic tube called the laryngeal mask airway (LMA) into the trachea. Then the anaesthetist and surgeon took over. We were free to stay and actually watch the operations but if anyone felt squeamish they could leave. Most of us watched them all – and without keeling over.

It was very good experience. I particularly liked seeing what was going on inside the patient during keyhole surgery. Via the camera, I could see what the surgeon was doing in there; snipping and sewing. It's fascinating. Surgeons have to be really good at needlework and it is important they don't pull the stitches too tight. In medical school they are encouraged to practise by darning old socks. One surgeon told me not to tell anyone that. And I haven't. I've only written it and he said nothing about writing . . .

The training provided by CHC was quite different to what we had done before, although along the same lines. We worked with Royal Navy and RAF rescue crews in COSARM, which is run by the RAF. It was a bit awesome trying to get to grips with different techniques but we had to catch up with new methodology. It was a tough three weeks training; in the classroom for most of the time, including Saturdays. There was intense theory along with practical procedures like cannulation. We now had to cannulate a buddy rather than practice in a hospital. I found the theory side of it pretty heavy going and then we had the paramedic intermediate exams. However, I got through it.

One of the bonuses of shift work is that there is lots of time off to do other things. Diving is a great leisure activity and I still do quite a bit of this with Michael Skelly. He still talks to me even though he is now very famous in broadcasting circles, after filming the vet plunging into the sea. We used to have our own boat, a 14-foot inflatable with a 20-horse Yamaha and I remember on one occasion, diving with him at Loch Leurbost. I was wearing a dry suit which had neck and cuff seals to ensure the person inside it stays warm, and as I left the surface and dived down, I put some air in my suit to counteract the water pressure. I just pressed a button as I descended and the deeper I went, the more air I had to put in.

On the way back up, I had a problem venting the excess air because the inlet hose had jammed in the on position. I tried two or three times to free it – no joy. There was an air relief valve on the shoulder of my suit and I managed to get my hand on that briefly, but the air was filling the suit faster than it was venting out and I started ballooning. The top of my suit was just one big bubble and I couldn't get my arms down to press the relief valve on my shoulder, this meant I was zooming up towards the surface with no control over my rate of ascent. It was a long way up and I was really rocketing. When I hit the surface, I came clean out of the water like a nuclear missile. That's if you can imagine a nuclear missile that looks like a Michelin Man. But that wasn't the end of it, I still couldn't get my arm on the relief valve on my shoulder, the inflation valve was still open and the air kept hissing out of my suit. I had never been in that situation before in my entire professional diving career.

Michael saw what had happened and came whizzing along in the wee boat, grabbed me, turned the valve off on the bottle and pulled the seal of my suit open, just as it was starting to choke me. That certainly wasn't a very nice experience, and to this day, I always make doubly sure about the maintenance of all diving gear. What happened to me could have had serious consequences had I been on my own, or Michael had been further away.

However well-trained at landing on decks the SAR crew were, there were other factors which meant we had little or no control over how landings were carried out during some rescues. We did also depend on fishing crews having some knowledge of helicopter rescue procedures and how they could help make landing quicker and safer for us. On the 25th of January, 1989, we had a tasking to a fishing boat, the Swanella. She was about 100 miles west of Stornoway with an injured crewman, and the coastguards told us they were sending a doctor down to the base. Dr Nigel Beresford arrived just as we were given instructions to take the casualty off, due to the injuries he had sustained.

She was a large vessel with a foreign crew. We had to decide whether to get me onto the bow or the stern. Due to the extreme sea conditions the vessel was sliding down the waves and we were losing it completely at times. It was far too dangerous to do a deck transfer on that heading so we asked the skipper to turn downwind and try a bow approach. This was a safer way to get the transfer done although we were actually flying backwards. We told the skipper of our intentions to use the hi-line and he said that he knew nothing about it – and neither did his crew. Oh, great. We decided to try and drop me on board without using the hi-line as it can cause all sorts of complications if people don't know what to do. It was a tricky manoeuvre to land on the deck, as we had to pick the right moment. I was winched out about 40 yards ahead of the bow and lowered down to a height that I was happy with. It's very difficult in high seas like that, when the pilot hasn't got much of a reference, but I indicated that I was ready to be winched on board.

The chopper started the run-in to the bow. I was signalling to the winch op with my hand to adjust my height but it was difficult. I wanted to get my feet onto the bow and stabilise myself rather than be dragged into the rigging. Almost in the water one second, the next I was up on the top of the mast, looking down onto the deck. The last thing I needed was to get entangled in the rigging before unhooking: that could rip your limbs off. I wanted to come in over the guardrail and get rid of that hook as soon as possible. We ran in again, but just when I thought the height was right I came in underneath the bow which came crashing down.

I ended up in the water and came back up like a drowned rat. Spluttering, and probably cursing too, I was pulled away. Signalling that I wasn't hurt, we started again. This time I was level with the top of the mast and, just as I approached over the deck, the whole boat rose up on a mighty wave and, crash, I found myself on the deck which had helpfully come up to meet me and made high-speed contact with my bum. That was just fine, however. I was where I wanted to be. No time to lose, I got the hook off immediately and ensured that the winchwire and hook were clear of any obstructions before it was retrieved back to the chopper. That was the first job out of the way. The second was to look after the casualty. I had to go in the bow door and into the accommodation block where I found some very agitated-looking guys cowering behind a door. With not a word of English between them, it was somewhat difficult to find out who the casualty was.

They took me to a guy who was actually walking. I checked him over – he had blood coming down the side of his face but I couldn't see much more amiss. After patching him up, he was walking wounded and I decided I was going to use a double-lift harness to get him off the deck. A double-lift is what the winchman wears as a safety harness and that's why I decided to use it, rather than a stretcher or a strop. Because of the sea conditions, I didn't want a stretcher being thrown all over the place with the guy inside it. He had on a lifejacket which I had taken down, along with the harness, and I had him ready to go in a few minutes. I don't think he understood very much when I told him we would be lifted together – he was pretty frightened. The other crew members responded well when I indicated they should help me take their colleague up to the bow, in preparation for being winched off. Radioing to the helicopter crew that I would be ready in five minutes, we went up to the bow. The boat had gone off course quite a bit because it had begun to roll from side to side quite violently and we got in touch with the captain again, to get him back on his original heading; that done, a hi-line was sent down. I hooked on with the casualty and, just at that point, the boat dipped down into the waves, the helicopter moved left and, whoosh, the two of us were gone.

I saw the bow disappearing on my right-hand side but we had a huge swing on because the blissfully ignorant ship's crew didn't have the gumption to control the hi-line, and the next thing I knew, there was a massive impact as we hit the water. We disappeared under a wave for two or three seconds – although it seemed a lot longer than that at the time. All this time the casualty was gripping my neck so tightly that I was almost choking and I had to prise his hands off me. We came back up to the surface and were winched into the helicopter. The casualty was safe and sound although somewhat petrified, and there was blood and sea water everywhere. The inside of that aircraft looked like a bomb site but we soon stopped the bleeding and he was none the worse for his ducking, although he was certainly a bit shocked. Dr Beresford then took over. We got back to Stornoway and the guy was taken to hospital where he made a full recovery.

The captain is, of course, the boss on a chopper. That said, on board search and rescue helicopters, at least the civilian ones, every crew member is involved in decision-making. We had the winchman, winch operator, the co-pilot and the captain on board and, if necessary, a medic or other specialist. What actually happens on a rescue also depends on the weather, the sea state, whether it's day or night, as well as the medical needs of the casualty. If a casualty looks like he may not make it then we are going to do whatever we can to try and get them off a vessel, while also bearing in mind that the winchman could be injured, and that the casualty could be hurt on the transfer as well. All these things are taken into consideration. In practise, the captain will normally ask the views of the winchman and the winch operator.

The crew would generally come to some agreement on what we were going to do. Often we'd say let's see how it goes and if it doesn't look too good, we'll bin it and rethink the plan. If a casualty broke a finger or was seasick, or was suffering from a non life-threatening affliction then, in heavy sea states, we would normally think seriously before putting the winchman down. There was no point in putting him at risk for little reason. If the winchman was injured on a non-urgent job there would be no rescue cover until someone else was found to stand in. At other times, we could be informed of someone seriously injured or, perhaps, a body on board. That can be quite a tricky one because the skippers of foreign vessels will often say they have someone who is seriously injured rather than dead. If there is no doctor available and just a winchman – who cannot actually pronounce a casualty dead unless it is an obvious fatality – skippers on these, mainly foreign, boats know that a winchman has to take the casualty with him, even though he knows the casualty is dead. We simply had to do that until someone qualified to do so pronounced him deceased. People didn't like talking about it but these were the situations in which we sometimes found ourselves. Skippers don't like lifting their nets as they are under pressure from the owners to keep earning money and they could be missing out on thousands of pounds worth of fish.

On the other hand, there were times when someone, for example, a crewman, had a broken wrist or very minor injuries – even no injuries at all – but just wanted home for a wedding, a funeral or to see his lass. The skipper would want to get them off the ship as they were of no use, or just not motivated. There would then be a phone call made to the coastguards from the owner, saying the casualty must be recovered from the ship because they were very seriously injured. We would go out in all sorts of sea conditions only to find the 'serious' casualty waving goodbye to his friends with a suitcase in his hand. We would get them onto the chopper – sometimes with great difficulty if conditions were bad – check them out for injuries and find nothing wrong. When asked what the problem was, we got the stock phrase, "I no understand Engleesh." On many occasions we took casualties to hospital who discharged themselves straight away and hopped onto the next plane out. These situations don't happen so much nowadays and there were rumours that concerns had been raised with certain foreign governments. We often felt we had been used as some sort of glorified taxi service – paid for by the great British taxpayer, of course.

Hoax calls usually come from children, drunks and, well, idiots. They don't usually come from responsible people like, say, members of Her Majesty's forces. However, we once were called on a bogus rescue job after emergency signals were picked up. When we traced the source we found ourselves slap bang in the middle of a massive, secret military exercise. It was in September 1990 that coastguards said someone was picking up a carrier wave: a radio signal without voice, and we were asked to investigate. Climbing up to a few thousand feet, we picked up a signal and told the coastguards it was coming from a south-westerly direction. They asked us follow it to see what we could find. Off we went, away down to west of Uist and Barra, and found ourselves in the middle of a large military

Cuillin mountain rescue, Skye 2005

Training with MV Isle of Lewis in the Minch

FV Jack Abry rescue in Atlantic

Myself and Ben the spaniel, without the grenade in his mouth!

View out of cockpit window, heading to Ben Nevis, 2008

Chris on the wire

L-R: Jimmy, Graham,Chris and Owen. Last job on YME, 2011

Our dive boat belonging to Michael Skelly

Stornoway and Stornoway Airport SAR Base

Night rescue from fishing vessel in the Atlantic

My friend, the late Tim Jarvis

exercise. There were aircraft carriers and fast jets everywhere and we got the distinct feeling we were not supposed to be there.

Our captain, Graham Lee, was getting stroppy radio calls from various ships. "Unidentified helicopter, you must leave this area now." Then the Ark Royal, no less, invited us to skedaddle, smartish, as we were mucking up their wargames.

Apparently, it was supposed to be a hush-hush exercise and nobody except the participants knew about it – not even HM Coastguard. All had been fine until one of the emergency beacons on a Type 21 frigate accidentally started transmitting. A fat petty officer probably sat on it. The strange thing was that the ship's crew knew nothing about the fact they were emitting distress signals that were being relayed by satellites around the globe. It doesn't say much for all their own detection systems that a radio beacon was set off, right in the middle of a fleet of the Royal Navy's state-of-the-art warships, and not one of them noticed a thing.

The coastguards and the rescue centre at Pitreavie were all picking up the signal. We were able to narrow it down and told the navy it was coming from HMS Ambuscade. Sheesh, they were really embarrassed about that. That was their cover blown for the whole exercise. Every man and his dog knew about it by that time. We had been talking to them on Channel 16, which every fisherman and boatman listens to. A year or two later, HMS Ambuscade was prematurely retired and sold to Pakistan. Oh dear – I do hope that had nothing to do with us.

CHAPTER 9

When you work on a rescue helicopter you come across a lot of dummies. No, I don't mean my lovely former colleagues, but dummy runs. Each individual situation has its own hazards. If we were replicating a rescue at sea we would first discuss the deck from a spot about 40 yards back from the port quarter. That's where we normally winch onto a deck after picking a landing spot. The captain would decide the helicopter's height, to ensure he was clear of all obstacles. Having chosen the spot, we would check engine power and start the practice run-in.

The winch operator would say, for example, "forward and right 20", "forward and right 15", "height is good, tail is clear", "speed is good" and so on. He would 'con' in the aircraft: that's just a conversation, so that the pilot would know the rotors were well away from obstructions and that the tail was also away from dangers. However, whatever height the aircraft was at, the winchman would normally be at a height of no more than 40 feet.

The winch operator would continue his patter until he was ready to plonk down the winchman. If the pilots were happy, they would say how much power they were using over the deck and they would discuss emergency procedures in case something went wrong. If a pilot lost engine power, for example, he would revert to those procedures and move away. He would never fly directly above a deck without discussing what to do if something went wrong, such as engine failure, what to do with the winchman, whether to cut the wire or whether to take him away with the aircraft, depending on the situation at the time.

It's up to the winch op and the pilots to press the shear switch to cut the winchwire, if necessary. In every dummy exercise, this is a normal routine to train for. Everyone knows exactly what is going on all the time. Nothing is left to chance. If, say, we had a casualty at the bottom of a cliff, we would do a dummy run above the area because there could be turbulence and we might not be able to get the winchman into position. This was always tested before any winching. On the mountains too, we would always go and have a look at the job first, check where the casualty was and test the air for turbulence. We did that with orange smoke flares which would show the wind direction. Sometimes we had to work in conditions which made it very uncomfortable for all the crew as the machine was buffeted all over the place. But that's part and parcel of flying around mountains and cliffs.

So how can a winchwire be cut? An explosive bolt is fitted into the winch itself. In fact, there are two winches and both have explosive cutters fitted into them. If the winchwire is caught in the rigging of a boat, for example, it may be necessary to cut the wire and the patter would then be "cut cut, cut cut, cut cut." The winch operator, the co-pilot and the captain each have a covered switch for cutting that wire. If, for any reason, the explosive cutter does not go off then the winch operator has a handheld cutter in the back of the aircraft, beside the door and, at a moment's notice, he can slice the wire manually. Winchwires have been caught on decks before and they can snap just like a piece of thread. They can then whiplash back up and damage the aircraft or the crew – or, even more disastrously, get into the rotor blades. I have seen the damage done to a military chopper after that has happened. Snapped winchwires can bring an aircraft down very quickly. If they don't, they can rip the winch off the side of an aircraft in an instant. In the past, winchmen have sustained serious injuries after being dragged through rigging. Not me, thank goodness. The winchman has a quick release fitting (QRF) on his harness which clips onto the winch hook. The quick release buckle is fine as long as there's no weight on it. You have to turn it and hit it firmly with your hand to be released from the harness.

Another vital piece of kit for any rescue aircrew is their tongue. The crew need to talk to each other before, during, and after each job. Debriefs after any rescue or training exercise were important; they were done when we returned to base, after the crew had cleared up the mess, all the search and rescue gear and medical equipment had been replaced on the helicopter and everyone had settled down. If it was 3am then we would leave the debrief until breakfast time. In actual fact, debriefs happened all the time: at work, at dinner and even in the pub. We'd go through exactly what we had done in the last job or exercise. We would all sit round a table and the captain would ask if everyone was happy. If someone was not happy about something they would have a chance to say so.

We would discuss what had been done in the training or SAR exercise and work right through each and every event that had happened. This could take anything from half an hour to an hour, and if someone was unhappy with the way things were conducted he would speak out and it would be discussed: what was not done that should have been done. If it was thought someone should have done something that they hadn't, then the issue would have to be properly aired. As I recall, we had another term for that collaborative performance assessment strategy. What is it again? Oh yes, it's called a bollocking.

Remember, we worked as a team and things were expected to go according to plan, as far as possible. All being well-acquainted and briefed for emergency procedures, be it at sea or over mountains, we knew that it was important to discuss even wee issues. If an issue wasn't mentioned, it could affect future teamwork. That is what a debrief is all about. Unfortunately, there are always some who think they know better than anyone else – and that's a bigger problem.

Even nowadays, despite media coverage, there are a lot of people going on to the hills who are inappropriately dressed and poorly equipped. Not too long after I started as a winchman, in the summer of 1988, we were called to the mountains of Kintail because there were some hypothermic people there. We were given a grid reference for the spot and found a group of adults and five young girls who were in need of rescue. They had been high up and did not have the proper clothing on, and were in a bit of a state, crying and feeling very sorry for themselves. I thought to myself, 'This just shouldn't happen.' But it does – all the time. People think because it's a lovely, warm day, beautiful blue sky, that they can just take a walk into the hills and they don't think of what could happen if the weather changes – as it often does.

These girls were on a course with adults who, quite frankly, should have known better. In that sort of situation, if we are not available and there isn't a mountain rescue team available, people are going to find themselves in serious difficulties. It's fine if you can contact people by mobile phone, but in those days you couldn't. One of the adults had to go down, find a phone and alert the authorities and that's how we were alerted to pick them up. There may be times, even now, when there could be a break in communication because of gaps in mobile phone coverage or whatever, and that's when a tragedy can happen and someone could die of hypothermia.

On that particular occasion everything worked out fine – the girls were taken to hospital, warmed up and were none the worse for their experience. But anyone going on to the hills should make sure they are well-equipped and well-dressed, and the mountain rescue team informed of their whereabouts. Those lasses had no waterproofs and were simply ill-equipped, regardless of the fact that it was the middle of summer. It was July 11th, but once you get a few thousand feet up into the hills, the weather can change to freezing rain and hailstones, even at that time of year.

When people saw a winch op, or other crewman, perched precariously at the side door of our helicopter, casualties and other observers would often ask us whether anyone had actually fallen out. In my time no one did, thankfully. The crew do attach themselves to despatcher harnesses, also known as monkey harnesses, which are anchored to the top of the cabin, precisely to prevent any unplanned descents without parachutes. However, in July 1989 we were looking for a missing walker in Loch Maree and were picking up mountain rescue and Search and Rescue Dogs Association (SARDA) teams to assist. We were getting a man and his pooch ready to be lowered onto a mountain top. The guy had his dog in a harness and we got them attached to the winch hook. We'd just got him lowered below the sill of the aircraft door when the dog slipped out of the harness and fell – all the way down.

That poor animal fell at least 20 feet. I just couldn't believe it.

The poor search and rescue dog, I think it was a collie, was lying on the ground and obviously hurt. We lowered his handler down and I thought he was going to pick the dog up and bring him back to the helicopter. Instead, he unhooked himself and started running away, dragging the injured dog with him. That poor animal had his back end bust. It was just awful to watch. The winch operator was Jeff Todd and he was absolutely fuming about the treatment of the injured animal. We manoeuvred the helicopter forward to try and get this gentleman's attention and signal him to bring the dog into the aircraft. He wouldn't even look at the aircraft and it took five minutes before he actually looked up and we got his attention.

I think the guy himself was just embarrassed. He was hoping that no one had noticed anything, but thankfully we managed to get him back inside, along with the dog which was quite badly hurt. This was one of the more unusual incidents that happened in the helicopter. Those guys are responsible for checking the harnesses of their own dogs in all aspects of a rescue. I don't know what happened to the dog but hopefully it got better.

SAR crews are the same as any other crews, whether they be military or whatever. Any time a group of people get together there is a chance they are not always going to see eye to eye; there can be a bit of friction and personality clashes. Of course, I saw this happen in Stornoway and, it would not be right for me to pass the buck here, I have been involved in some sharp exchanges myself. Stuff happens in the SAR world. Personal stuff as well, which has nothing to do with SAR but which can bring about clashes between strong personalities. Something may have happened in the pub at the weekend, for example. These conflicts would sometimes come up at work and could cause a bit of friction, on and off duty. As long as people had the common sense and a sense of responsibility, to leave issues aside during work, they would not escalate.

I remember when I was training to be a winch operator there was quite a mix of ex-Royal Navy and ex-RAF crew on the Stornoway base. I started off my winch op training really to enhance my skills in navigation, etc. There's an awful lot involved in being a winch operator on a SAR chopper and, while I won't go into it all just now, maybe I can just touch on the training aspect.

The Royal Navy really does have a different way of working from the RAF. I was on shift one day with an ex-Royal Navy winch operator training me, teaching me all the different aspects of navigation, different ways of using the computer and so on. We then had an overland navigation exercise, a NAVEX in the lingo, to get us from point A to point B. It was necessary for me to talk to the pilots all the way through this exercise and tell them what I was doing. It went well – I was a quick learner back then. The next time I was on shift, I was with an ex-RAF winch op; I began to carry out the same procedures in the same way and all of a sudden the exercise came to a halt.

He said, "Chris, do you not remember how I trained you the last time? You've gone and changed it."

Had I? I thought to myself that he was losing it, or I was. The lecturing about how I was doing things the wrong way continued until we got back to base and I was feeling pretty unhappy about being told off constantly. We had the debrief and I sat there red-faced, wondering how everything had gone wrong. It turned out, of course, that the root cause of all the confusion, and me being blamed for ignoring my training, was down to the differing ways in which my instructors were trained themselves, by the Royal Navy and the RAF respectively.

The first winch op asked, "Who the hell taught you to do it that way?" I explained I had been taught to do it that way by the last crew. "Ah, yes, but that's the RAF way of doing it. This is the Royal Navy now." No it wasn't. There I was, piggy in the middle, getting blasted from all sides when it wasn't my fault at all.

The clash between cultures is not so bad nowadays. The differing methods of training were officially recognised and now both the RAF and the Navy do the same job in the same highly professional way, but new aircrew are trained up in a different fashion. So, for the last few years that I was working, if anyone outside the military had to be trained up as winchman or winch op, they were sent to RAF Valley in Anglesey to be trained. So there is now a standard type of training that is used and which is followed – and a good thing too.

Searches for missing people or vessels normally go on for a long time. However, as with any job, the time will come when you must call a halt. It's really up to the coastguards to decide when to stop any ongoing SAR rescue jobs, whether that be their own rescue teams, the ground teams or the helicopter crews. They make the call that there is no hope of anybody being found alive. Of course, you'll always find people who live in the local area where a tragedy has happened, who will continue searching, not just for a few days or a few weeks but for months, in the hope of finding even a body that can be buried by a family.

Unofficial searches can go on for a long time. After an official SAR had been called off, we would often go to that area on training missions and continue searching for bodies, until such time as we decided ourselves there was no hope of recovering anything, or anyone. Of course, it is good for the relatives of those who are missing to see that there are still people searching for their loved ones, long after the formal, full-scale search has been called off and I believe the RNLI do the same.

A typical example was back in 1996, when a boat from Stornoway called the Sovereign hit the rocks at Rubha Reidh on the west coast mainland. The crew was picked up by an RAF helicopter with one lad still missing; Jimmy McCulloch, who was also from Lewis. His body has never been recovered but the search went on for some time afterwards until the coastguards called a halt to it. The helicopter crews and, I am sure, the lifeboats, were still scouring that area, as were people from Stornoway who were going across in fishing boats to search the area.

If I had a couple of days off, myself and John 'Iosdaidh' Macleod would head across with our diving gear and we'd search all the gullies and little caves in the hope of finding Jimmy's remains, to take him back home. Unfortunately, it was not to be. The helicopter continued winching guys off fishing boats and putting them into the search area for a few months until everyone was pretty sure they had searched every place that they possibly could; on land, on sea and under the sea, all around that coast. The remains must have been washed out to sea and were never going to be recovered. When that happened, we felt for all the families concerned. These desperately sad events occur at sea – and will happen in the future.

*

Contagious illnesses can cripple the effectiveness of the crews of a rescue helicopter. Plans are always made for such eventualities but I suspect they don't work very well nowadays. In days of yore, when I was on the S61, there was a reasonably good system. Back then, most of the crew lived in the town of Stornoway, or close to it. Very few of the crews actually live there now, because they do two weeks on and two weeks off when they go back down south. That is why the age-old practice of trying to get someone to cover for you on shift is now pretty difficult, I imagine. Going back to my days, if you were sick or injured, and this happened a fair bit, word was sent to the coastguards and to the senior winch op, Steve Branley. He would phone around to see who was available to stand in. That could happen at any time, and obviously if someone had been to the pub with the boys then they couldn't volunteer. If someone was not going on shift the next day and, even if they were, shifts were changed to fit in with whatever was necessary.

When it came to preparing and training for the severest weather conditions, we were just thrown in head first and told to get on with it. In reality, it depended a lot on who the captain and the crew you were with on shift. There are, of course, training limits laid down in the operations manual for SAR and this sets down the conditions you're allowed to train in – particularly the wind strength and sea state. If you are going to work in extreme conditions, such as around cliffs and on mountains on a regular basis, it is absolutely vital that crews undergo training in just those conditions. I have trained in some very wild conditions at sea, a decision taken entirely by the pilot and crew, of course. Someone could always turn round and say they were not going to do it in hazardous conditions but in practise, training has to be done as a team. If the team decision was to go along with the captain then the exercise would happen. I am not talking about taking ridiculous risks and getting into dangerous situations. That would be a non-starter in a training situation but if, say, the weather was bordering on extreme conditions then those are the very conditions in which lessons can be learned properly.

Much more can be achieved by getting out there than by sitting in a classroom talking about how to do something. Common sense was what was needed. We ran through virtually everything we would do on a real-life search and rescue mission in heavy seas, for example. Such training has to be done from time to time but obviously there are debates to what extent we should simulate extreme conditions. As far as I am concerned training should be done as realistically as possible because that is certainly how techniques and procedures became second nature to me.

There were occasions when I would go to work long before my shift started. Was it because I was very keen? No, not really. I was keen for most of my time in the job but the main reason was to walk the dog on the beach. There were also times when we all went to work late, usually when we were given the heads-up by the coastguard or somebody at the base, perhaps the secretary or one of the engineers, that the outgoing shift were still away on a job.

Now and again it was necessary to push the capabilities and the endurance of the aircraft, and of ourselves, to the limit. We did this quite a bit actually, to try and achieve a successful outcome for any SAR mission but there were times when we would go outside even those normal limits in certain conditions – flying in a storm or during hurricanes. On long-range jobs, calculations would be worked out by the onboard computers, taking into account factors like wind direction, wind speed, transiting time and fuel burn. The problem with winds is that they can change unexpectedly. When they do, all calculations are out of the window and things stop going as you had so precisely planned. We always had to have reserves of fuel – a big long-range fuel tank. In practice, this was only needed for rescues way out in the Atlantic and we always had to be acutely aware at all times of onboard fuel levels. Only by doing this, can a crew know how much fuel is needed to get to the scene – and, just as crucially, whether there will be enough fuel to get back to dry land. As well as fuel, there are many other factors which have a bearing on the outcome of a rescue mission when you have to get to a place where a boat is on its way to the bottom, or you're trying to pick people out of the water.

A typical example of this was the Hansa which has been mentioned earlier in the book. We rescued nine people after she went down about 200 miles south west of Benbecula. The wind had veered – and not to our benefit – and we knew we had only a matter of minutes to complete the rescue, and return. It's a very difficult decision to pick up half a crew and leave another two or three in the water to certain death. Should we leave them there or should we pick them up, knowing that if we do, we may not have enough fuel to get back to base? Sometimes there would be an oil rig out west where we could refuel or, instead of going directly to Stornoway, we could divert to Benbecula when that was a shorter and safer option. That was the kind of situation where we really pushed ourselves and the aircraft to the limit – and perhaps a little bit more.

If you're in heavy seas, you're maybe a good bit off land and the helicopter captain or the winch op is telling you that you've only five minutes left before having to depart for fuel reasons, and you still have to get the casualty up on deck, well, you've got tough decisions to make. You cannot hurry if the casualty has spinal injuries – they cannot be rushed onto a stretcher just because the helicopter has to return for fuel. What usually happened in these cases, if we weren't hundreds of miles offshore, is that the winchman would radio the captain suggesting he should return to base, pick up more fuel and, by the time they returned, the casualty would be ready for winching. That happened to me twice, and I was left on fishing boats with casualties until the chopper came back after refuelling.

If we started moving casualties with spinal injuries around in heavy seas there was a possibility we could make the injury worse and perhaps paralyse the casualty for life. Having said that, if a casualty did not have spinal injuries but was in a life-threatening condition, the right decision could be to get that person off the vessel as soon as possible or he could die. That decision had to be made by the winchman down there on the deck. Whatever he decides at that time rests with him. Whatever is said afterwards at a hospital, it is always the winchman's decision to lift the casualty off, or not. The helicopter crew may get in touch with a hospital or a doctor on shore and ask for advice on the matter but it's the guy at the sharp end who normally has to make these decisions, and if somebody's life is slipping away he has to make the decision fast, get on with the job in hand and hopefully at the end of the day it will prove to be the right one.

We once had a man with spinal injuries on board a vessel out in the Atlantic; he had fallen down the hatch into the hold. When I went down to put him onto a spinal board and fit the stiff neck collar to immobilise him, he said he couldn't tolerate it. I thought at the time it was because of the injuries he had sustained, but he explained to me he had a condition called osteoporosis – he had brittle bones. The disease meant he held his chin down to his chest all the time and he couldn't wear a stiff neck collar.

I padded him up as best I could without the collar because he simply could not bear it and it was affecting his respiration. We put him into the stretcher and back into the helicopter before taking him to Raigmore Hospital in Inverness. On landing, while passing the casualty to the ambulance, I explained to the paramedics why the casualty was not wearing a collar. This information obviously didn't filter through to the A&E department in Raigmore because by the time I got back to Stornoway, the hospital had been on to the chief pilot demanding to know why the casualty's neck hadn't been properly supported. I passed the information on to the chief pilot, including the fact that I had briefed their paramedics, and it came back that they had failed to pass on the information. Apologies were forthcoming and it was eventually understood that he had osteoporosis and had been looked after properly.

On the mountains, anyone who has had a fall is likely to have spinal injuries and they can be serious. In these situations, if the winchman is first on scene he will give the casualty the once over and carry out a full body check as best he can, depending on where the casualty is located. It could be a narrow ledge or a cliff, for example, where these procedures really cannot be carried out. Depending on what kind of weather there is, he may be asked by RCC or the coastguards to have a look and see if it's possible to get the casualty out. If we were in any doubt at all we would get in touch with the mountain rescue team who would have already been alerted. If there's something a winchman cannot deal with himself, then he should get the mountain rescue team there as quickly as possible.

There are times, perhaps in the middle of winter, when it's blowing a snowstorm and you can only see a few feet in front of you and you might have only one chance of getting in to a casualty. If the casualty is perhaps so hypothermic, or so badly injured, that they have to be taken off straightaway, that would be a decision which would have to made. We would consult with the mountain rescue team and make a decision there and then. By the time we picked up the MRT, it could be too late.

The chopper would always hover into wind as far as possible. If we were hovering over the back of a vessel, or in mountains, if there was a puff of wind we would try and hover into it. This relates to the power ratio of the helicopter itself. If the chopper doesn't hover into wind it will lose power; the engines will still be operating at full revs but the aircraft will not get much lift. Helicopters fly better in some wind rather than none at all.

There's also definitely a feeling that some aircrew work better in the mountains than others. You will find this in both military and civilian services. Some pilots can read the mountains like a book. They know exactly where the wind is coming from and they are on top of it all the time. I remember on one occasion, Tim Noble, the deputy chief pilot in Stornoway, turned round to Captain John Bentley one day and said, "John, I believe you're in league with the devil."

What he meant was that John Bentley was really good at reading every puff of wind, the direction and strength, and he knew exactly where every demarcation point was going to be. He would say things like "be prepared to get a buffeting in five seconds" on a particular part of the mountain, maybe about 300 feet away from the edge. Sure as hell, it would happen. John seemed able to anticipate the downdraughts and updraughts better than most. Ach, maybe Tim Noble was right enough in what he said.

Mountains too, can be a real challenge to helicopter rescue. Every peak and every corrie has its own quirks and dangers. Often, we would hover over an area one minute and the next, the wind had changed and we would have to fly away out of there and try again somewhere else. The pilot would lower the helicopter slowly to an area like a ridge, all the while making sure he had enough power to safely do so, with the winch op checking rotor clearance and talking him down to the spot. Often, in narrow areas, it was even necessary to carry out a balancing act on one or two wheels to give a chance for the MRTs to clamber in or out. That way, the pilot had a reference, the aircraft was stable, for a short time at least, and it was a safer way to get personnel in and out of the chopper. It just depends on the circumstances in the mountains at the time because, believe me, the weather can change very quickly indeed, up there.

While I'm talking about how dangerous mountains can be for flying and landing, I should stress that every pilot who goes to the mountains is well trained to do so. They appreciate the dangers involved in penetrating low cloud, and turbulence on the hill. Low cloud can come down in the mountains very quickly. Sometimes we would be trying to get from A to B, maybe through a glen, to find a casualty or mountain rescue team, and we would discover the weather was closing in behind us, or in front of us. Crews should always be aware about the state of the cloud. A pilot trying to get through into the next glen will sometimes spot an opening in the cloud. That is a phenomenon called a letterbox, also known as Sucker's Gap. Risks occurred when the pilot was going for the gap and it suddenly closed up. If that happened, we had to have an escape route planned to climb to a safe altitude while avoiding the surrounding peaks. Working among the picturesque but jaggy mountains of the north of Scotland is no place for a faint-hearted aviator.

The number one priority in Stornoway was obviously not the hills but maritime rescue. That's the reason the chopper was put there in the first place, although we did a lot of training for both types of jobs. Almost on a daily basis, we looked for ships and fishing boats to take part in maritime rescue exercises. The pilot would get the chopper near a moving fishing boat, a moving deck as we called it, and with the winch operator, carry out a dummy run to ensure that all our procedures were safely executed and everyone was happy. Then the chopper would return and move in slowly to lift the winchman aboard a clear area of the ship, normally the port quarter of the vessel. Regular passengers on Caledonian MacBrayne ferries will have seen this procedure being carried out from the stern, I'm sure. That ferry company was very good in allowing us to use their ships for training purposes in the Minch.

On the hills, we didn't train all the time in snow and whiteout conditions because that type of weather didn't actually happen very often, unless we headed to the mainland mountains. However, even on training exercises, we would find people on the mountains who required our services, which only enhanced these exercises for us. In situations where we were looking for a casualty, low cloud could rapidly cause problems and we sometimes had to abort the search and let the MRT teams do their stuff. They could search for the casualties and take them back down below cloud level so that we could then fly them to hospital. Of course, when we were doing rescues and training of that type, we would carry our own bag of medical equipment which included pain-killing gas, bandages, splints, stretcher and needles. This type of training had to be done on a regular basis with the mountain rescue teams, who are also trained to a very high standard in medical care. That made our job much easier.

We had a safety equipment store at the base for re-supplying the aircraft and personnel with whatever gear might be needed at a moment's notice. My other job, apart from being a winchman, was to look after the gear in what we called the safety equipment room. That meant lifejackets, rescue strops, suits, beacons and harnesses. All these items of equipment had to be maintained on a regular basis and logs had to be kept. I had to take a course in Aberdeen to get a certificate for this.

Only two of us were qualified in the work – Gerry Flannery and myself – and it took up a lot of time, especially when gear had been immersed in salt water. We would wash all the equipment in fresh water, take everything apart, clean and if necessary, grease and oil, then hang the equipment up to dry. Sod's law being what it is I would be in the middle of doing this when we would get a call-out to a rescue. It is essential that the gear is maintained for safety reasons. However, it is a thankless job.

We had two helicopters at the Stornoway base, both Sikorsky S61Ns. The spare helicopter didn't have much rescue gear on board, but if one aircraft broke down or needed an engine or gearbox change, then all the SAR equipment would be transferred to the other chopper. The engineers, however, used to work all through the night to change engines or gearboxes. They were a very professional bunch of lads.

Every Sunday, the duty crew would go on board the chopper and scrub it out. No, there were no cleaners for the helicopter. We were the cleaners and we worked hard; we had to look after it. The engineers scrubbed and polished the outside of the aircraft and we got down on our hands and knees to scrub the floor, the walls and the ceiling. It would be sparkling by the time it was finished. We would then change the batteries in the defibrillator and the radios. When that was done the helicopter was ready for the shift taking over at 1pm. If there was no time to clean the chopper, because we were out on a rescue for instance, it wasn't a problem because the next crew would do it. It was, however, frowned upon to forget and leave it for some other crew to do.

The winch wire on which I dangled, and to which I trusted my life, was about 300 feet long. There is quite a palaver when it is initially fitted to an aircraft because it has to be tightly wound onto the winch drum. In fact, it has to be so tight that the technique was to attach a 600lb weight to the winch hook and the helicopter would then climb to 300 feet. It would then slowly descend, with the 600lb weight being slowly winched in to make the wire taut on the drum. That had to be done by the book and on a regular basis, according to the manufacturer's instructions. Winch wires are very special apparatus to winchmen, for obvious reasons. If anyone had any doubt about the wire or the winch, it would be checked out and, if necessary, changed right away.

Each person on board the aircraft was responsible for navigation. We had an ops room at the base with maps and charts and if the coastguard scrambled us, they would give us a position and any other relevant information they had. We would pinpoint where it was on the map and decide which route to take. It wasn't always a straight line. There could be doglegs through glens, turning back on ourselves and very often we would have to go and pick up a mountain rescue team on the way.

Navigation is one of the most important aspects of the job. We had computers on board which would do most of the navigation for us just by keying in a 'lat and long' or a way point. The computer would then fly the aircraft and take us to our destination. However, we could never totally rely on this. Like anything else mechanical or electronic, it could fail. If the computer went kaput, the winch operator would take over and leave nothing to chance. Once in the mountains, the task was map reading, using the Mark 1 Eyeball, and maps to cross terrain. That was when the winch op was the main man. However, even then, it was not left to just one man, as the pilots were also map reading and the winchman would be trying to locate any heat source on the infra-red camera. Navigation offshore is also is done with computers but, as always, is continuously backed up by a real live human being.

Sometimes our training with Forward Looking Infrared Radar (FLIR) would involve the winchman guiding the aircraft up, say, Loch Erisort, Loch Ewe or some inland sea loch. The pilots would be following the winchman's instructions or patter, but closely monitoring instruments, while the winch operator would be map reading up front. And if at any time, anyone was unhappy with the exercise then a pre-planned escape route would be followed – all in a relaxed, controlled fashion. It was intensive training; talking the pilots through each manoeuvre while confirming height, speed, rate of turn and avoidance procedures. You had to have confidence in what you were doing. FLIR cameras are normally used for locating heat source, for example, missing walkers, but on many occasions we successfully used them in night mountain rescue operations. It's a good piece of kit.

As I have mentioned previously, we carried a fair bit of gear on board, all essential for SAR. This included stretchers, thermal blankets, a spinal board for immobilising people with neck or spinal injuries, oxygen, Entonox gas for painkilling, as well as medical bags and vacuum splints heat packs, a flare gun, and wire cutters. One of the other items we used to carry on board was teddy bears, and a lot of people wondered why we did this. We had a large bag of teddy bears in the back of the aircraft and made sure it was full all the time. They were there because from time to time we were going to get young kids as casualties on board this big noisy aircraft. Sometimes all these kids had to do was look at me in my big yellow helmet – like some giant wasp – and they would burst into tears right away.

We also carried boxes of chocolates on board for the crew and casualties, and some soft drinks and water. The water was multipurpose.

If we picked up divers suffering from the bends, we needed to get fluids into them intravenously and also give them water orally. That can greatly help a diver with the bends. The other equipment always on board included heart defibrillators, blood pressure monitors, lifting strops and high lines and the list goes on . . .

Wet winching is something we did on a regular basis, whether for training purposes or for real, when a person ended up in the water. To pick someone out of the water, the winchman had to be lowered down to the surface with his legs in the water, depending on sea conditions. This would help him gain control of his own heading. He was then trawled towards the casualty, something that is not very easy to do in heavy seas with two rescue strops on your arm. These are canvas strops which fit round the casualty, under the arms and under the knees, to enable him to be lifted into the helicopter along with the winchman. This is known as a hypothermic pick-up. It keeps the blood in the core of the body and is the preferred method of pick-up whenever possible. The training for this was done in Broad Bay, near Stornoway Airport, on a regular basis.

We worked with the mountain rescue teams regularly. This was also part of SAR training and normally on a Sunday, when MRT volunteers were off work, we would meet at their MRT base for a safety brief or even, occasionally, out on the mountain. We would have a chat, make a plan and transport sometimes up to 20 of the team to various locations. Each team leader would be in radio contact with their base and also with us, and we would aim to enact full rescue scenarios.

We trained with the coastguards as well, of course. There are teams in Stornoway and other teams all over Scotland whom we worked with sometimes. They would pick landing sites for us on a field, or some other uncluttered place, and identify it with an orange smoke flare. We would sort out some kind of exercise and fly the teams to out-of-the-way places, such as on the coast. Sometimes a dummy would be hidden on a hill or a coastline and the search would continue until it was found. The MRT members would also get a helicopter safety brief as a refresher, involving the use of rescue strops and hi-lines.

At times we were called out to people a long way offshore who might have suffered amputations or falls into holds on ships. Or perhaps the person had suffered a heart attack. The winchman would go down with all his gear and, if there was time to patch someone up on board the ship, he would do that. If not, the casualty would be picked up in what's called Scoop and Run – when we got someone up into the helicopter as soon as possible, and off to hospital. The winchman would have a much more stable platform inside the chopper to work on the casualty and this also saved time, which is very often a lifesaver.

If I'm telling my life story, I should put in most of the stuff that bears revealing – even if it is a tad embarrassing. And slightly face-reddening it was too, the day I had to be rescued myself. It wasn't actually a proper rescue and I suppose I just used my contacts to get me out of a sticky situation. Many summers ago, a few of us went out to Loch Langabhat. I was with a friend, Calum Gillies, or Hoggles as we know him, fishing for salmon. All legal and above board, of course. We didn't catch many, but we had a good time fishing that day. It was smashing weather, a good breeze, so it was fantastic fishing weather. We slept the night in the bothy beside the loch. It turned really calm at about 4am the next morning and as the sun rose, the midgies came out.

Well, I've never seen or felt midgies like that in my life – apart from the rescue in the glens. It got so bad that we couldn't do anything outside. Some of the guys had midgie nets but they were not much help in a cloud of bloodthirsty midgies. Even they couldn't go out, so we had to confine ourselves to the bothy as we discussed our next move. Two of the lads had quads, but myself and Calum had walked in from the road. After a long discussion, the lads with wheels decided to head off; if they got a bit of speed on then they could leave the midgies behind. Us poor souls left behind were wondering what on earth we were going to do. We hoped the wind would get up about midday but, no, it remained flat calm. I was sure those beasties were breeding in the heather as we spoke. There were more and more and we were, literally, being eaten alive.

They were so bad I had only one thought in my head and that was to get out of there. It was a hot, sticky day so walking wasn't an option, because of the heat and the distance to the road – we were just outside Scaliscro Lodge. I had my mobile phone with me and I ran up to the highest point to see if I could get a signal. I got in touch with the pilot who was on duty that afternoon and explained our predicament to him. I asked him, if the crew was in the area on a training exercise, would he please consider lifting us two poor souls up from the bothy at Langabhat and taking us back to Stornoway. Please? That's exactly what he did and that was how Calum and I got out of that situation – we were both very grateful. Thanks, John. After that, I made sure to keep an eye on the weather when planning any further fishing expeditions to Loch Langabhat, or anywhere else for that matter, to ensure the weather wasn't going to be as calm as it had been that day. The experience was just soul destroying, knowing it would have taken a very long time to get to the road, by which time we would have been red raw and undoubtedly in need of hospital treatment. Thank goodness for the helicopter.

CHAPTER 10

When my longtime employer, Bristow Helicopters, lost the contract for search and rescue in the middle of 2007, and the Canadian company, CHC (Canadian Helicopter Corporation), won the contract, with the helicopter Sikorsky S92, there was a lot of work to do in preparation for the changeover. We had to learn a lot about the new aircraft and the transition took some time, but the guys at our base were fast to learn and we just had to get on with the job in hand.

How were these two workhorses of the sky different? It was like going from a very comfortable saloon car to a very fast sports car. It was a rougher ride; the helicopter was built more for speed and power. The S92 had crashworthy seats placed in the port and starboard side of the aircraft, two long-range fuel tanks in the rear and a very impressive-looking ramp at the back which could be raised or lowered by the pilots, as necessary.

The equipment we used was also different in that it was more up-to-date, but we soon got used to it. The way we approached rescues, how we were winched in and out of the aircraft, the seating arrangements, it was all new and we had to learn new techniques. The downdraught from the new helicopter was absolutely horrendous. It affected our operations when winching underneath the aircraft and using the stretchers. It was a completely new ball game, with strong turbulence causing stretchers to spin quite wildly and, on one or two occasions, the chopper proved to be downright dangerous when the winchman and stretcher were violently thrown upwards, denting the underside of the aircraft. We had to develop methods in our training to cater for getting out of situations which could cause problems. The learning process took a while but we got there.

My first proper SAR job on the S92 was a fisherman with a hook in his eye, on 24th October 2007. He was on the fishing vessel, Spinningdale, which came to grief on St Kilda not long after that. It was a month after that before I was on my next rescue and, guess what? That too was a fisherman with a hook in his eye. The Spinningdale came to a sticky end during a really bad storm one night. I'm not sure if it was engine failure or some other cause, but she ended up on the rocks on Village Bay, St Kilda, in atrocious weather conditions. The S92, piloted by Liz Forsyth, the first woman captain at Stornoway, went out there that night in horrendous weather conditions. They managed to winch the crew clear of the Spinningdale which was battered to bits against the rocks. They did a fine job and were presented with awards for the rescue that night.

In search and rescue, the crew has to be available for long shifts but that doesn't always mean they will be working hard throughout the whole shift. In all my years, on both types of helicopter, we were rostered on 24-hour shifts, from 1pm until 1pm the following afternoon. We were a four-man team and, if we were not out on a job, just got on with what had to be done, whether it was maintaining SAR equipment or the other really exciting task – scrubbing out the aircraft. Shift personnel varied all the time. A crew could only work so many shifts before having time off, so each crewman worked with different captains, co-pilots and winch operators all the time.

We had many false alarms but they were mostly well-intentioned. On October 5th, 1988, a crew consisting of Alan Elphinstone, John Bentley, Vic Carcass and myself were sent to the tidal rocks at Gress, on the east side of Lewis. Someone had spotted a person in yellow oilskins waving their arms, obviously in distress and probably stuck on rocks. At first glance we couldn't see anyone at all. There were a couple of seals swimming around and many seabirds, but there was nobody there. We went right down to the side of the low-lying rocks but there was nowhere that anyone could have hidden. We searched and thought the informant must have been mistaken. We returned to base and had been back for about half an hour, having shut down the helicopter, when the scramble bell rang again. The coastguard again said, "Scramble to the rocks at Gress."

Yet another person had been spotted in yellow oilskins, waving their arms and stuck on the rocks. This time I was winched down onto the rocks and I searched every nook and cranny on the reefs at Gress. There was nothing to be found although I did get a very strange feeling there. Why were people seeing a person in yellow oilskins on these rocks and I couldn't see anything? Looking in the same direction as the informant was, out to sea, there was nothing. No boats behind the rocks, nothing. That job definitely gave me a spooky feeling as I went back to the helicopter and flew back to base. We discussed it afterwards with the coastguards and, to this day, we don't know what those people had actually spotted on the rocks. It still gives me a bit of a shiver to think about it.

A familiar term to us SAR crews was CRM, or 'crew resource management'. It is reckoned that a lot of accident and aircraft crashes happened in the past because there was no crew resource management – which is just really about how crews communicate. Don't be bossy on board and don't ignore any comments from your three colleagues, in case they are important. It's all about talking to each other, understanding each other and getting on as a team. It may work for some people but there are obviously some types who don't take it seriously and just laugh at it. These are the people who are difficult to get along with sometimes. There is a good reason for CRM. It does work.

Like most other bases, we had health and safety awareness drummed into us. We were taken down to the hangar and a ladder put in front of us on the ground. "What should you do with this ladder?" we were asked. Yes, move it away so someone doesn't trip on it. Just common sense. We were told we must apply these principles throughout our working lives. Er? The obvious question for the instructors was how should we apply health and safety in a helicopter, in a raging storm, 100 miles offshore, or in the mountains, when dangling on a wire while being whacked off the side of a ship, or in the water, near propellers and looking death in the face? They would just look at me with a smile on their faces and wouldn't say very much, implying that obviously certain aspects couldn't apply to our working lives all the time. As far as I am concerned, health and safety is common sense which should be applied by each and every individual. However, I don't think we need to be shown in ridiculous detail how to look after ourselves all the time. It is pretty obvious to most people what health and safety should be about. My own personal view is that health and safety is out of control. I don't think health and safety comes into it out in the Atlantic; crews look after each other in the best way they can. If they get hurt, they get hurt. That's all there is to it.

A doctor would often volunteer to come along when we were going out to casualties who we knew had been seriously hurt, or had grave medical conditions. This was normally Dr Brian Michie of the Group Practice in Stornoway. We took many medics over the years but Brian was the regular on-call doctor. He is trained in using search and rescue equipment and has been on many missions. In fact, he received the MBE for his services.

If there were very rough seas and we were a long way out, we would definitely try not to put the doctor down on board the vessel because doing this took up so much more time and fuel. In those circumstances we would try to scoop and run, get the casualty on board as soon as possible and help Brian to look after them as we headed back to hospital. When we were involved in tragedies, we often felt it deeply. Personally, I am not ashamed to say I was reduced to tears on one particular job – it involved the drowning of young children. I knew there was nothing we could do but there was still this sense of helplessness, sitting in a multi-million pound chopper with all its lifesaving equipment onboard, all to no avail. We still had to act professionally – but inside we were absolutely gutted.

Why does anyone do a job where they face regular danger? Being a winchman can be a dangerous job. But not all the time. You accept a level of risk when you start work on an SAR base. You know in your head that sometime soon you will probably find yourself in danger. On a hill, on a stormy sea, it's going to happen. There is no point in spouting off about it being a horrible, dangerous job and wishing you hadn't taken on the job. If you have that attitude then you really shouldn't be doing it in the first place. Of course, you get butterflies in your tummy a lot of the time. You know you're going to be hanging onto that wire and that you will feel fear because you don't know if a massive wave will suddenly rise up and crash you into the rigging of a vessel that could chop you in half. That possibility makes the best winchman anxious. You also know that the training you've had, and which the guys in the chopper have had, is going to ensure there is much less chance of that actually happening.

Having been on many fishing boats in the course of my dangling career, I have often wondered about the people who do that job for a living. Maybe, it has been suggested to me, I would want to be a fisherman myself when I finished on the chopper? How can I put this? No. In fact, no no no. There are not many jobs, especially more physical ones, that I would not tackle. However, I have a lot of relations who have been fishermen and who were at sea all their lives. My father was a navy man and I too, had sea in the blood, and as a kid spent time on a fishing boat with my relations in Marvig, when we were on Lewis. That was an exciting time for me then, but looking at the job nowadays, there is no way I would work as a fisherman myself. Over the years, many fishermen have said to me, "Listen, thank you very much for the job you do," after we have dragged some poor guy out of the water and maybe saved his life. Well, that's just what we were there for. Fishermen are the special guys. For SAR crew, it's just the job we do to pay the mortgage, to put bread on the table – and fish, of course.

In my humble estimation, fishermen who fish for a living have the most challenging, cold, dirty, wet, yucky and downright dangerous job that's going. No doubt about that. I came to this conclusion after many years winching up fishermen with all sorts of injuries. Yep, far more dangerous a job than mine. My task was just to hang on to the end of a wire from a helicopter to pluck them to safety. I got thrown about a bit now and again, but it was rare that I was very concerned for my own safety. Whenever I have met fishermen, in the pub or on the deck of a storm-tossed boat that we have gone to assist, I have found them to be some of the most unassuming people you could ever meet. I completely respect them for what they do. They were all physically able lads who could turn their hands to many other jobs but still they did that one. Somebody's got to do it if people are going to have fish on their tables but, oh, hell, it's a hard life. There are all sorts of dangers a fisherman can face at sea. Like winchmen, they too get thrown about, but on board a vessel the chances are higher that they will break limbs – or worse. I have come across all types of horrific injuries on vessels, from amputations to severe burns; guys half-drowned after being dragged overboard, to say nothing of hooks in eyes and abdomens, internal injuries, spinal injuries, severe sickness, dehydration and hypothermia.

To be quite honest with you, there are just so many things which can go wrong on a fishing boat at sea in violent weather, or even in calm for that matter, that it is a really risky business. As well as the usual dangers like sinking, collisions and groundings, fishing boats also go on fire regularly. That's a horrendous situation when it happens. When a fire breaks out on board, it tends to spread rapidly and the chances of everyone escaping completely injury-free are often miniscule. When things are good with the fishing, they are very good indeed and there is good money to be made. But things can deteriorate and go wrong rapidly at sea. If you are a long way from shore, where the best fishing tends to be, it's probably going to take some time before a rescue helicopter or a lifeboat actually gets out there to help you.

There was the odd time when, yes, I did think to myself I was going to die on a job. More than once, to be honest. There have been situations, mostly in violent storms at sea, where I have thought, if this mast, this rigging or these propellers hit me, I will not make it out in one piece. It's a bit of a strange feeling, not that I ever resigned myself to it definitely happening. I was there to do a job; it was what I was trained for. I fought back. No, I wasn't going to let the old Grim Reaper get a hold of me quite yet. You've just got to punch him in the eye and say, "To hell with you this time. Try again another day, mate."

Flashes like that have gone through my mind, but only for a split second because there are always too many other things to contend with, apart from the Grim Reaper. Am I religious? Put it like this, I am not a disbeliever. My parents, who are both gone now, were very religious. As a youngster I had to go to church every Sunday, whether it be in Dornoch or in Marvig, although I have to say that a two-hour Gaelic service didn't turn me on to religion very much because, well, I didn't understand a single word. Having said that, I was brought up with faith and there have indeed been times, and there probably will be again, when I would say a wee prayer to the Big Fellow in the sky.

Knowing any rescue could be my last, I did make arrangements in case the worst happened. I had a will made. I did all that a long time ago – it would have been very silly of me not to. The unthinkable could have happened to me – or to anyone, at any time and you have to think of your family. Setting out my last will and testament, and putting matters in order, gave me a sense of calm.

Since I came to Stornoway in the mid-1980s, my life has been a rollercoaster. Although I miss my home town of Dornoch, I will always remember that the only reason I came here was because Shona, my wife at that time, was transferred here by the police. When the job with Bristow Helicopters came up, that was the beginning of the major high points in my life so far. The training, and then qualifying as a search and rescue helicopter winchman for Her Majesty's Coastguard was certainly that. Anyone who is, or has been, a helicopter winchman: military or otherwise, knows the adrenalin that pumps through the veins, the sheer excitement of a job with a good result. Everything involved in being a winchman, even the continuous skills updating, the medical training, and, of course, the camaraderie was fantastic.

In the early days, socialising was as crucial a part of the job as the rescues. Chief pilot Alan Elphinstone used to host barbeques at his home with marquees, food: the works. We had Christmas parties at the Caberfeidh Hotel in Stornoway which were also a way to get to know many people in the town. For those who were on duty, Alan would hold another bash later, so nobody lost out. They were fantastic times. We all lived in the town then. Unfortunately, I don't think many of the SAR crews live locally now. The big parties are gone and there is a different approach to work and socialising. It's all part of you, even that big lump of metal – the Sikorsky chopper.

Dozens of crewmen have come and gone over the years, from pilots to co-pilots, winch operators and winchmen. Some of these guys are sadly no longer with us. I am thinking now of my old friend Jeff Todd, whose ashes were spread over the North Sea by an RAF helicopter because he was an ex-RAF man.

He was one of the guys who taught me in Stornoway, along with ex-Fleet Air Arm crewmen Smiler Grinney and Steve Branley, who is retiring as I finish this book. These are the guys who trained me up and got me ready for the job. I have to remember how privileged I was to be trained for the role by such experts, who so eagerly helped me be part of such a great, highly-skilled unit.

I also want to mention my friend Tim Jarvis. He was a member of the East Sutherland Rescue association and also of Dornoch Coastguard, who, sadly, died after falling ill during a routine exercise with one of the RAF Lossiemouth helicopters in October 2004. Tim collapsed while on board the Dornoch inshore rescue boat and was pronounced dead at Raigmore Hospital in Inverness after being flown there by the helicopter he had been on exercise with. Tim is believed to have suffered a heart attack. He was a dental technician who moved to Dornoch in the early-1980s, and he left behind his wife, Sandra, and daughters Lynn and Sara, a family on which he doted. We had a lot of things in common and I found Tim to be an absolute gentleman, and very professional in whatever he did. I will miss him very much.

I was in Search and Rescue for 21 years with the contractor Bristow and then another final year with the latter operator, CHC Scotia. Among the good times, there have been some sad times as well. Inevitably, there has been loss of life on jobs we were on. However, if just one person in those 22 years is alive now because we appeared in the big noisy whirlybird, then that's a bonus, and I think there are many.

When we rescued people and took them back to their own families, it was the greatest feeling on earth. Some think, of course, that we professionals don't have feelings at all and that we are trained to deal with whatever is thrown at us but, deep down, I personally have very intense feelings. Whether I was called to help fishermen, mountaineers, ladies in labour or whoever, I did not feel any of that so-called professional detachment. I felt for them all. I think most helicopter rescue crews feel this more than they would admit to. Don't get me wrong here, I am not casting aspersions on people like mountain rescue teams and lifeboat crews who do an absolutely fantastic job.

My search and rescue days are now over. An injury to my arm on a mission in November 2003 caused me problems for years afterwards. I had to have two operations to repair my elbow and to try and sort out nerve damage. The injury happened while I was landing on the deck of the French trawler, Jack Abry, in a storm, about 70 miles north of the Butt of Lewis. After the last op failed, the specialist in the hospital told me that I could not continue doing such a job any more. I therefore had no option but to leave in early 2009, after 22 years service.

I can never go back to the job again. This saddens me because I do miss the camaraderie and life at the base. On the other hand, there are more politics surrounding the service and the contractors nowadays. It would seem that, in the future, SAR may not even be run under the auspices of the Coastguard, Royal Air Force or Royal Navy, but by faceless bureaucrats. As I write this, it has just been announced that my previous employer, Bristow, is to take over all helicopter search and rescue in the UK. There will be no military SAR helicopters and it is expected that experienced RAF and RN crews will quit the service and join Bristow.

Many people have mixed feelings about giving the sole responsibility to a private company – and an American one at that. Even Prince William told Prime Minister David Cameron not to go as far as handing over everything to one company. Other experienced mountain rescue people have pointed to Bristow's excellent track record in Stornoway and elsewhere. Of course, it is all about wonga. The government does not want to spend money replacing the ageing RAF and RN Sea King choppers. The new contractor has vouched to use the new S92 machines that I worked on in my final couple of years. They are more powerful, faster, better-equipped and can operate much further from base.

The RAF and the Navy are going to feel the loss acutely because it has been such a vital and public part of their work. It leads me to think that I've been involved in the golden years of SAR. I certainly won't miss the internal politics, but I will always miss the thrill of being called out on a search and rescue mission, and dangling from that wire.